Pub Walks
in
The Mendips

Rod Lawton

Published by Sigma Leisure – an imprint of
Sigma Press, 1 South Oak Lane, Wilmslow, Cheshire SK9 6AR, England.

British Library Cataloguing in Publication Data
A CIP record for this book is available from the British Library.

ISBN: 1-85058-310-2

Typesetting and Design by: Sigma Press, Wilmslow, Cheshire.

Maps by: Orbit Design

Text photographs: Rod Lawton

Cover photograph: The White Hart, Cross (Rod Lawton)

Printed by: Manchester Free Press

General Disclaimer

Whilst every effort has been made to ensure that the information given in this book is correct, neither the publisher nor the author accept any responsibility for any inaccuracy.

Preface

Pub Walks in the Mendips is not a book for serious walkers. Neither is it a book for real ale fanatics. Really, it's a book for people who enjoy country walking and are not averse to the odd jar and perhaps a bite to eat after two or three hours of exercise.

Having said that, some of the walks do represent a fair old challenge for the unfit and overweight, and the infirm, too. Elderly folk and children may find the longer walks too much for them. There are plenty of stiles on the Mendips, too, and unless you're reasonably supple you might have some difficulty with them. And you need to be fairly sure-footed. There's no shortage of mud in the countryside and there are a few stiff, rocky climbs to negotiate.

Does all this make it sound as if hill-walking on the Mendips is only one step removed from a Himalayan expedition? It's not, of course, and there's nothing in this book that couldn't be tackled by a reasonably fit walker. The shorter walks are ideal for children, too, but you may have to watch them near cliffs, animals and main roads. Indeed, a country walk makes a great family outing, and I've kept a special eye out for pubs that welcome children.

Experienced walkers may find some of these routes a bit 'tame'. I make no apologies for that since they're meant to be recreational diversions rather than tests of sheer stamina. Anyone interested in the latter should get hold of a booklet called *West Mendip Way: The Walker's Guide*, by Derek Moyes, which is available from most local tourist offices. It describes the West Mendip Way, a 30-mile route established in the jubilee year, 1977, between Uphill and Wells and taking in most of the sights of the Mendips.

In writing this book I have made one rather sweeping assumption – that many of the people reading it will be visitors to the area. To all those who live round here, I'm afraid I'll spend a lot of time stating the obvious. There may be things you didn't know about the Mendips, though, that you'll find out in this book. (I'm sure there will be lots of letters from historians telling me things *I* didn't know, too!). And I hope there will be many Mendip residents who are encouraged by this book to get out there and explore these hills.

I've chosen the walks in this book primarily for their scenic value. The Mendips are not the most famous range in the country, but they surely offer the most variety, including dramatic clifftop paths, windswept moorland, deep, dark forests, babbling brooks, picturesque villages and even sweeping seascapes.

And that's not all. The Mendips have been heavily populated since Roman times and before, and have a great deal of 'history'. And even when these remnants of the past have become either overgrown or long since buried, the sites remain and the stories and legends that surround them are fascinating.

While I've tried to include as much historical detail as possible, naturalists may be disappointed. I'm afraid I couldn't tell a Larch from a Spruce, and while I can just about distinguish a rook from a buzzard, I wouldn't care to test my ornithological skills any further.

As far as pubs are concerned, I have my own tastes and I'm sure you have yours. Not all Mendip pubs are the same, and there's a wide variety in this book. They range from rather fancy hotel/restaurants with excellent menus, to cramped, stone-floored pubs with beer served from a trestle table behind the bar. I started this book with some vague notion that walkers preferred typical 'quaint' country pubs. I soon realised that, just as I didn't want to write a book solely for rucksack-toting hikers whose idea of a walk *starts* at ten miles, neither did I want to write a book for beer snobs.

Instead, this is a book aimed at folk fed up of staring at the landscape through a car window and above the heads of hordes of tourists. People who want a few lungfuls of country air, wide open skies and panoramic vistas, and a satisfying, relaxing refreshments afterwards.

Rod Lawton

CONTENTS

INTRODUCTION

The Mendip Hills   1

Walking in The Mendips   3

Mendip Pubs   9

THE WALKS

Around Weston   **13**

Uphill Hill   1.5 mls   15

Brean Down   6 mls   21

Weston Woods   4 mls   27

Sand Point   7 mls   33

Hutton   3 mls   39

Around Bleadon   3 mls   43

The Western Hills   51

Brent Knoll	4 mls	53
Banwell Hill	3.5 mls	61
Crook Peak	7 mls	67
Dolebury Camp	4 mls	73
Around Shipham	5 mls	78
Around Axbridge	2 mls	84

The Mendip Lakes   89

Chew Valley Lake	6 mls	91
Litton Reservoir	2 mls	97
Blagdon	5 mls	102
Compton Martin	2 mls	108

The Central Mendips   113

Black Down	8 mls	115
Burrington Ham	4 mls	123
Cheddar Gorge	6 mls	129
Around Priddy	5 mls	137
Stockhill Plantation	2-4 mls	144
Westbury Beacon	6 mls	149

Around Wells   155

Wells	5 mls	157
Wookey Hills	5 mls	164
Ebbor Gorge	3 mls	169
Around North Wootton	3 mls	175
Glastonbury Tor	7 or 3mls	179

The Eastern Hills   187

Mells	7 mls	189
Nunney Combe	2.5 mls	195
Holcombe Church	3 mls	199

LOCATION MAP

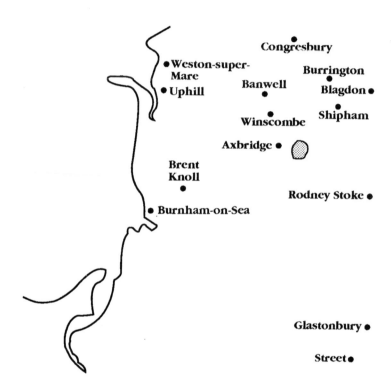

Chew Magna

Compton Martin

Litton Midsomer Radstock
Norton

Priddy Chewton
Mendip

Holcombe Mells
Frome

Wells Nunney
Wookey
Shepton Mallet
North Wootton

The Mendip Hills

The precise area defined by the 'Mendip region' is open to interpretation. I think of the hills as forming a long, narrow triangle tipped on to its side. The 'point' of the triangle is at Weston-super-Mare, and from here the range slowly widens eastwards, producing northern and southern slopes, with flat, raised upland in between. By the time you get as far east as Cheddar, you've seen the most dramatic scenery. From here eastwards the hills become more gentle and undulating. The Mendips effectively cease to exist as a discreet range of hills by the time you reach the base of the triangle (with Radstock at the top corner and Bruton at the bottom).

The Mendips don't boast too many truly picturesque villages because they're nearly all working communities rather than tourist attractions. Mells is very pretty, though, as are Rickford and Compton Martin. For the most part, however, Mendip villages are unexceptional. Most are either dowdy farming communities, or rural settlements overrun by burgeoning commercial centres. The remainder are tourist traps of the worst type – like Cheddar Gorge.

Much of the Mendips has been taken over by the Forestry Commission for the growing and harvesting of conifers. Coniferous forests tend to be gloomier and barer than their deciduous conterparts, but the Forestry Commission tracks and bridleways are always well-maintained and easy to follow.

Which is more than can be said for walks through deciduous woodland. These can be muddy, indistinct and overgrown – but still very rewarding. Bridleways are the best-marked routes, but also the muddiest.

Most of the rivers on the Mendips flow underground, thanks to the soluble limestone geology, so there are no great surface rivers to admire. However, Mells Stream is very picturesque, and Blackdown Springs in Rowberrow Warren is pleasant to walk alongside.

For most walkers, though, walking is all about hills. On this basis, the Mendips don't appear to score very well. Their highest point is a mere 1,000 feet. However, they rise steeply above flatlands which are barely above sea level, so the contrast can be quite striking.

The western end of the Mendip range is just that – striking. Brent Knoll is only some 450 feet high, but it rises out of an utterly flat landscape like an extinct volcano. And the highest hill on the Mendips, Black Down, still offers the sort of windswept moorland walking you'd expect to find on the wilds of Exmoor, not in the middle of Somerset. There's also excellent moorland walking to be had along Wavering Down, next to Crook Peak – one of the high spots of the region. And although the hills above Cheddar are only a few hundred feet high, the cliffs in the gorge fall sheer for their full height down to the road, up to 450 feet below.

There are snags, though. The Mendip region is a pretty densely populated area, and has been for centuries. As a result, it's well served by roads. *Too* well served for the keen country walker. Here I was faced with a dilemma. My instinct was to keep off the roads as much as I could, choosing cross-country routes where possible. At the same time, taking this too far can mean absurd and pointless diversions and even missing many of the sights you're doing the walk to see. I've reached compromises which I hope everyone will be happy with. Where possible, the routes stay away from roads. Where necessary, they use them.

Finally, when giving directions by road, I've stuck to two principal starting points – Weston-super-Mare and Wells. Anyone with a road atlas, though, will have no trouble finding these walks from any other starting point.

A road atlas is an optional extra, but an OS map is an essential companion. Sheet 182 from the Landranger series covers nearly all of these walks; Sheet 183 covers the far eastern Mendip area. You'll need an

OS map to accurately pin-point the position of each pub (though you'll also be able to find these from the directions) and, more importantly, to do the walks with and to use as a reference. Instructions on how to use grid references are printed on the maps.

Walking in the Mendips

The typical length of a walk in this book is four to five miles. The longest is eight. There are many of around two miles. In general, the shorter the walk, the easier it is. Novice walkers should bear in mind that a five-mile walk across country is NOT the same thing as a five-mile walk on pavements or roads. Walking across country takes about 25% more energy and about 25% more time. It may also be impossible to cut your walk short, should you get tired.

And how fast do you walk? It makes sense to find out, because you need to know when you're going to finish your pub walk, if only not to miss last orders! If you can walk at around four miles an hour on roads without too much discomfort, expect to cover about three miles an hour over the hills.

Having said that, it's best to assume a walking speed of about two miles an hour for these walks. There are two reasons; (a) you want time to take in the scenery, (b) navigation can sometimes be a challenge!

Navigation

National Trust properties are seldom difficult to find your way around because the paths are clearly-defined and signposted. In other areas, though, you're sharing the countryside with farmers. Footpaths are public rights of way, but they are also crossing private property, so you must not deviate from the marked route – except that the routes are not always marked! Farmers have little or no interest in maintaining public footpaths (unless their crops are threatened) and are not averse to locking gates that shouldn't be locked, blocking stiles with barbed wire and generally being unhelpful towards walkers.

It helps to have a Pathfinder map of the area when walking across fields. These maps are very detailed, even to the extent of showing you which side of a hedge or fence the footpath goes. This information can be crucial, but cannot be included on the larger-scale OS Landranger maps.

Where footpaths are signposted, the signs will usually take the form of a small arrow painted on a stile or a post. Note the direction the arrow points carefully, because the next stile may be 400 yards away across a field, and half-hidden by vegetation. It's easy to get off the beaten track, especially if it's not really beaten at all in the first place!

There are certain tricks you can use to stay on the route. Look at the map and try to select landmarks you can aim for. Distant hills, church spires and even trees can be highly useful when you have to resort to 'dead reckoning'. When crossing fields, look out for breaks in distant hedges – these can indicate stiles or gates. If in doubt, follow the field edge so that you don't miss the exit.

Above all, remember that your map is your best friend. If you get lost, don't panic. Don't trust your 'sense of direction' to get you back on the right track, either. Instead, take a long, calm look at the map. Then look at the countryside around you. Try to pin down as exactly as possible where you are, and then try to identify some landmarks to aim for. Only then should you set off again – usually in a completely different direction to the one your instincts had told you!

The maps printed in this book should get you through the walks without too much trouble. However, it's always good insurance to carry an OS map with you too. The best one for the Mendips is sheet 182 from the OS Landranger series (sheet 183 is a useful adjunct for the eastern end of the range).

While the Landranger maps show all the public rights of way, the Pathfinder maps are more useful still. They show field boundaries – very useful indeed for those navigational Bermuda triangles that appear in heavily-farmed yet seldom-trod areas.

But you'd need to buy about six Pathfinder maps to cover the Mendip area completely. This would cost you around £20! Try to find the cash, though, for the Cheddar and Wells maps. These cover the bulk of the walks and the trickiest areas.

If you do carry a map around with you, a plastic case is a good investment. The Pathfinder maps in particular disintegrate readily when exposed to rain, mud and perspiration.

Unfortunately, OS maps don't identify stiles and gates, yet finding these is the key to navigation through farmland. Our countryside is covered with footpaths and public rights of way, many going back centuries. However, just because they're public rights of way, it doesn't mean that people use them. Ordnance survey maps make no distinction between paths used daily by kids going to school and routes last used by eighteenth century peat-diggers.

Most, however, are reasonably well-maintained. But many (too many) can be very difficult indeed to follow. A well-used track cuts a visible swathe through pastures, moorland and woodland. An infrequently-used path leaves no such visible trace, and you must look for signs like stiles and gates in distant hedgerows. On open ground, look at the map and try to choose a landmark to aim for. And in woodland be especially careful. You can't 'invent' a path through woodland. Nineteenth century explorers used machetes and teams of bearers to beat a path through the African jungles. You have no such luxuries (unless you have some small children who can be pressed into service) and Mendip woodland can be equally impenetrable.

Most Mendip footpaths are signposted at the start and finish and usually at various points along their length. Signposts can be six-foot-high wooden posts, small, circular plastic plates on gates or arrows painted on woodwork. But then there will be occasions when there are no signposts at all. Indeed, it's not unknown for farmers to obliterate, obscure and even uproot them.

Farmland can present the worst navigational problems for walkers. It's usually pretty obvious from looking at the map and the countryside ahead of you where you want to get to – but it's how you get there that's the problem. Hedgerows are designed to be impassable. Fences and walls are built to be unscalable. Therefore you have to rely on finding gates and stiles.

Generally, a footpath will cross field boundaries via stiles. Some, though, take you through gates, and it's here – principally – that you can hit trouble. Farmers frequently lock gates that shouldn't be locked. They also put up lots of 'PRIVATE' notices. Unfortunately, there's no law preventing people from putting up 'PRIVATE' signs over a right of way. In the case of these Mendip walks, there are no occurrences of this. But if you decide to invent your own routes, you may come across it.

Ultimately, though you have to remember that farmers are trying to make a living in very precarious circumstances. They are subject to the whims of the weather, the Ministry of Agriculture and Brussels bureaucrats. Having tourists tramping all over their land (even if they're allowed to) is yet one more thing they don't want – but at least it's something that they can control.

Most farmers are reasonable, pleasant people. Just make sure you're reasonable and pleasant when you meet them. As far as locked gates are concerned, they're not much harder to climb over than most stiles. It doesn't do the gate's hinges much good, but that's the farmer's problem. Obstructions can be harder to get round. But if you're sure of your route you're perfectly entitled to demolish them.

Clothing

The Mendips can be cold, wet and windy in spring and autumn, and positively arctic during the winter. Walking tends to warm you up but, even so, it's better to be too hot rather than too cold. You'd have to be pretty foolish or pretty unfit to run the risk of exposure on the Mendips, but since progress may be slow when you're navigating through a tricky patch, don't rely on the warming effect of the exercise to offset a lack of clothing.

Wear lots of thin layers rather than a couple of thick garments. It keeps you warmer and it's easier to strip off progressively as you get hotter. Waterproof coats and anoraks may keep the rain out, but they also keep perspiration in. You end up just as wet (on a mild day) and twice as hot!

An umbrella is a much better bet. They're a bit tricky to handle in wooded areas, and you may feel you look a bit of a fool, but on open ground they really are unbeatable – they can also double as walking sticks when the rain stops.

Save the expensive specialist walking clothing for more ambitious walking expeditions in fiercer parts of the world.

In the summer, many of the hills are overgrown with bracken, gorse and brambles. It might seem pleasant to go walking in T-shirt and shorts, but it doesn't take many encounters with the Mendip vegetation to convince you otherwise. Particular local specialities include triffid-sized nettles, brambles like steel cables and gorse clumps like inside-out pin cushions; long trousers are always a good idea, even in the height of summer (*especially* in the height of summer).

Boots

About a third of these walks can be done wearing trainers or ordinary shoes. But the rest can contain sections which prove quite impassable without half-decent walking boots. Waterproofing is a secondary factor – the primary ones are ankle support for rocky paths and generous tread for slippery slopes.

You can waste a great deal of money on walking boots, and not necessarily by paying a lot for them. Cheap walking boots are poorly made, uncomfortable and don't last well – but they still cost more than a decent, sturdy pair of brogues. Expect to pay towards £100 for decent walking boots and, if that's too much, go for a decent pair of outdoor shoes.

Whatever you wear on your feet, take a spare pair of socks. This isn't to ensure personal freshness, but to save your feet from blisters if they get soaked. Because, despite what all the manufacturers say, there's no such thing as waterproof boots or shoes. Stand in a stream for a few moments to prove it. Or walk through a field of tall, wet grass.

Food & Drink

If there's one thing that will perk up a flagging walker it's something to drink and a bite to eat. But then if there's one thing to slow them down in the first place, it's a heavy rucksack...

By all means take something to eat and drink with you if you wish (as long as you don't spoil your appetite for the pub), but in my opinion none of these walks are long enough or arduous enough to make refreshments necessary. Rucksacks make you sweat in summer, even if they're nearly empty and stuffed pockets are cumbersome and can cause painful chafing.

My motto is, travel light. Unless you're a keen photographer, all you need is this book and an OS map. Anything else will slow you down and get in the way.

The Countryside Code

Finally, there are a few things visitors to the countryside should remember. Most are common sense, but they bear repeating.

Public footpaths are public rights of way across private property. Just because you are allowed to cross a farmer's land, it doesn't mean you are allowed to explore it. Don't stray from the path, in other words. Trespass is illegal. It can also damage farmers' land and crops – and hence livelihood.

Litter is also damaging. It's not just unsightly, it can harm farm animals. They can choke trying to swallow it, or injure themselves getting caught up in it. And someone, sooner or later, is going to have to clear up after you. It will almost certainly be the farmer, and he is not going to keep a welcome in the hillsides for the next party of walkers he meets.

Litter can, of course, be caused by carelessness. And carelessness can cause much more serious hazards – like forest fires. In 1957, 150 acres of forest was destroyed by a single fire in Rowberrow Warren. Forest fires start easily, but they're a darned sight harder to put out. At best, they leave acres of precious woodland a charred ruin for decades. At worst, they can kill. DON'T start fires in forests unless you know how to build them and put them out. DON'T throw away smouldering cigarette ends as you walk.

You don't have to drop litter or cause fires to be a nuisance, though. Many farm animals go for days without human contact, and it's very easy to make animals bolt. They can escape from fields and on to roads, run into fences or ditches and may even turn on you if particularly frightened.

People are usually pretty considerate towards farm animals, though (they view each other with similar misgivings). Children and dogs are different. Children because they don't know any better, dogs because it's their instinct to hunt and attack. Watch them both!

Above all, treat the countryside and its occupants with respect. It belongs to all of us, but not all of us rely on it for our livelihoods.

Mendip Pubs

The Mendips aren't a renowned walkers' paradise like the Lake District or Snowdonia, so there's not much of a walking industry here. Which means you get no typical 'walkers' pubs. What you do get is an enormous variety of watering-hole. At the upper end are places which are popular for an evening meal out – these are not necessarily overtly posh, but they are tastefully decorated and can be more expensive – not the sort of place for a boozy sing-song. Then there are those which are bright and breezy locals' pubs which also do a holiday trade. The beer isn't adventurous and neither is the food or decor. But these places are clean, neat, reasonably-priced and quite tolerable. And then there are the real country pubs. Not quite spit 'n' sawdust territory, but not far off.

There are few pubs where you get the 'freezing stare' on entering the door, because everyone has a car these days, and everyone likes to get out in it – even in the deepest, darkest depths of the Mendips, folk are used to seeing them there strangers frum the city quite often.

There are, admittedly, a few real dingy dives on the Mendips whose gloomy interiors are inhabited by centuries-old tobacco smoke and toothless cider-drinkers, but they're not included in this book!

However, the best 'rustic' country pubs are. The prime example of which is the Crown at Churchill. Its labyrinthine interior has stone floors set at various levels and gradients, wooden furniture designed before the invention of tape measures or spirit levels, and beer served from barrels lined up on a trestle table behind the bar. Marvellous.

What makes a good pub? Tastes vary, and so do the pubs on the Mendips. I've tried to pick the most presentable examples! In each case, though, the walk is the important thing – I haven't compromised too far on the routes just to incorporate a particular pub.

Most pubs offer both a lounge and a public bar, although in some cases the differences aren't all that obvious! If you're especially grimy after an arduous walk, the public bar is going to be the best bet. While publicans welcome the business, they don't want mud on their carpets.

If you're out walking with youngsters, you obviously want pubs with children's rooms – or at least bars that accommodate children if you're eating meals. Most pubs now do one or the other.

Most pubs also have very convenient car parks, but if you use a pub car park, make sure you use the pub too. Publicans, quite rightly, get distinctly miffed if people use their car parks but don't drink their beer. In the event that you do want to do the walk but don't want to visit the pub, where possible I've indicated alternative nearby parking.

I haven't gone into a vast amount of detail about the beer and food on offer for one good reason. Menus and beers – and landlords – are always changing.

'Ambience', or 'atmosphere', is a very important thing in a pub but practically impossible to describe. I hope, though, that by the time you've read the descriptions of the pubs you'll be able to form your own impressions.

Oh and there is one other thing – if you want to visit a pub, make sure it's open when you get there! Time your return with pub opening time or thereabouts, so that if you're delayed along the way there's still time to get a drink and a bite when you get there. There's nothing more soul-destroying than finishing a long, hard walk and having to drive home tired, hungry and thirsty because you arrived at the pub too late. I know.

Common courtesy

The Mendips are not a renowned walking area, so few pubs are set up to cater *specifically* for walkers. Which means that publicans will not be used to the sight of mud-splattered hikers in clumping boots throwing their coats and rucksacks all over their chairs. Don't do it!

(Having said that, many of the country pubs are used by farm workers, who are likely to arrive in a far worse state than a hill-walker...)

I always carry a change of footwear in my car. Many of the Mendip walks can get muddy, and mud that's clinging apparently securely to your boot when you walk into a pub will reliably detach itself at some point during your stay, and deposit itself on the landlord's carpet.

If you don't have a change of footwear with you (I really do strongly advise it), clean your boots up as much as possible before you go in and use the scruffiest seating area. It would be diplomatic, too, to disguise walking boots by pulling your trouser legs out of your socks.

It's not that Mendip publicans are hostile towards walkers – quite the reverse! – it's just that they wouldn't welcome farmers straight out of a cow field or building labourers straight off the site, either.

Through all this I'm assuming that you intend to travel in small parties. If there are a dozen or more of you, though, I strongly recommend calling the pub in advance if you all want to eat. The publican may not go as far as setting aside tables for you, but at least he or she will be able to make sure they've got enough staff in the kitchen that day. A sudden overload of customers in an already busy pub can be a nightmare.

And just as you shouldn't use a publican's car park when you're not using their pub, don't use a pub's garden facilities when you've brought your own packed lunch. I spoke to one publican on my travels who told me he once had a party of 13 arrive who, between them, spent £6.50 at the bar. They then proceeded to eat packed lunches and drink (for the most part) their own drinks on his seats outside.

That's not only rude, it's a waste of a good pub!

Around Weston

The Walks

Uphill Hill	From The Ship Inn, Uphill (ST 318584)
Brean Down	From the Brean Down Inn, Brean (ST 297570)
Weston Woods	From The Commodore, Sand Bay (ST 329633)
Sand Point	From The Long John Silver, Sand Bay (ST 332646)
Hutton Hill	From The Old Inn, Hutton (ST 350587)
Around Bleadon	From The Queen's Arms, Bleadon (ST 340570)

The Area

The Mendips are usually thought of as an inland range, but in fact at their western end they meet the sea – even jut out into it. Brean Down, the whale-like promontory stretching over a mile out into the Bristol Channel, is part of the same geological formation which makes up the rest of the hills. Just a few miles to the north, on the other side of Sand Bay, is a similar, though smaller promontory – Sand Point. Both of these offer excellent, varied and spectacular coastal walking.

The Mendips meet the sea at Weston-super-Mare, a faded Victorian resort which has alas seen better days. Especially since it has now developed into a major commercial centre and become the focus of much of the region's housing developments. Nevertheless, the town has its own attractions for walkers – particularly Weston Woods, on the ridge to the north of Weston, separating it from the villages of Kewstoke and Sand Bay. Weston-Woods are a large deciduous area well endowed with tracks and signposts. The Woods also house the remains of Worlebury Camp, an ancient Iron Age hill fort that was in its day probably the best-defended on the Mendips.

And although Weston threatens to engulf many of its outlying villages, there are still unspoilt and fascinating country walks within easy reach of the town. At its southern end is the village of Uphill. Although now tiny by comparison, Uphill is a much older settlement than Weston-super-Mare. The Romans used it for shipping out the lead they mined deep in the Mendip Hills and since then the village has also been the scene of Danish raids and, later on, the smuggling of contraband.

A little to the south of Uphill is Bleadon village, also associated with heroic tales of thwarted Danish invasions and the site of an ancient Celtic settlement, while to the west is the village of Hutton, at the base of Hutton Hill. From here you can walk through the secluded Hay Wood up towards the 'Roman Road' (thought to form part of a direct route from Charterhouse to Uphill) and then down through tree-lined Canada Combe.

Uphill Hill

Route: Uphill – Uphill Marina – Uphill Hill

Distance: 1.5 miles

Start: The Ship Inn, Uphill (ST 318584)

By car: Uphill is on the outskirts of Weston-super-Mare. From the town centre, head for the sea front, then south to the Uphill turn-off. Follow this road until it curves round to the left, and take the right turn-off at this point. Follow this road through the village, then turn left at the base of the hill. The Ship Inn is about 200 yards away. There's limited pub parking space, but roadside parking isn't a problem except at busy times.

The Walk

This is the shortest walk in the book, but I make no excuses for its length. It's easy enough for the young children and older folk, with limited climbs, but offers plenty to see in an ancient settlement with a very colourful history. It centres on Uphill Hill, a striking landmark at the southern end of Weston-super-Mare.

The village itself dates back to the Roman occupation, and features a Norman church and 13th century windmill as well as more modern attractions like a thriving little marina.

The place probably gets its name not from the hill that dominates the southern side, but from the ninth-century Danish raider Hubba, and the word 'pill', meaning 'creek'. Hence, 'Hubba's Pill'. Before that, the Romans named it Axium. They used to export Mendip lead from here at the time of Christ. It was still being used as a port in the seventeenth century. By now the trade was in lead, zinc and iron, plus cattle, sheep and various staple goods. There was other, illicit, trade too – Uphill was very popular with smugglers, as was much of the Somerset and Avon coastline.

Really, it's only recently that the sprawling Victorian seaside town of Weston-super-Mare has taken over, threatening to swamp Uphill in the process. Even so, Uphill was still the site of the first real attempts to promote the spot as a seaside resort (at the end of the eighteenth century). It failed, alas.

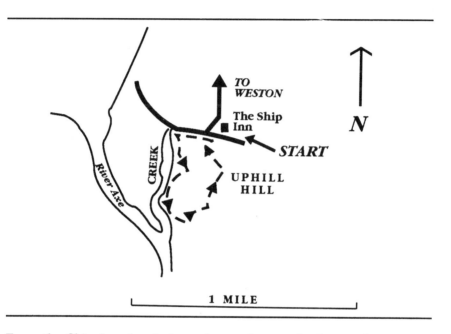

From the Ship Inn, head along the road towards the sea front. After about 400 yards you'll come to the entrance to the marina on your left. This is protected by substantial concrete flood defences after freak tides several years ago caused serious flooding and a great deal of damage. This area has one of the highest tidal ranges anywhere in the world.

Incidentally, the beach at Uphill has a very shallow slope. This, combined with the high tidal range, means the sea races in at quite a speed. Be very careful not to park your car below the high tide line for any length of time!

Also, don't be fooled by the proximity of Brean Down, just across the mouth of the river Axe. It looks close, but the grey mud which surrounds the river is very deep, and very, very dangerous. It is completely impossible to cross by foot. Try it, and you'll end up being fished out by a helicopter – if you're lucky.

Uphill marina: The marina lies on a small creek of the River Axe below Uphill Hill.

After that, perhaps we won't visit the beach after all! Instead, walk left through the main gates into the marina and ahead of you you'll see a fenced-off enclosure. The main track leads off to the left of this enclosure. Instead of going this way, though, turn right. The path here isn't too well defined, but you can't really go too far wrong. Photographers should note that this is an excellent spot for sunsets, with the looming bulk of Brean Down on the skyline and the rippling water in the creek to reflect the colour of the sky. There are derelict boats, to photograph too, with weathered wood, rusting chains and once-gaudy paintwork to capture on film.

You soon reach the corner of the wire enclosure, and here you should look out for a couple of steps over a stone wall to your left. Head left here and carry on walking along the river's edge (creek, actually).

Beyond the boatyard is an artificial lake which is very popular with budding windsurfers and canoeists. To the left you get a good view of Uphill quarry, and its low, but dangerous, cliffs.

From here, follow the track along the low dykes by the river's edge, heading towards a low mound. When you reach it, turn left to head back towards Uphill Hill, walking clockwise around the base of the mound. You shortly arrive at a gate in a stone wall. Now just head straight uphill.

Uphill Hill is a fascinating place. It's dominated by two ancient structures. The first that you come to as you climb up the hill looks quite bizarre, like a small turret that's somehow become separated from its castle. It did in fact start life way back in the 13th century as a windmill. Since then it's also served as a watchtower through the centuries. In 1934 it was rebuilt as an observatory – the Royal Observer Corps used it during World War Two – and it was refurbished during the '80s to make a vantage point for taking in the surrounding countryside. An iron stairway takes you up to the roof, where plates set into the wall point out the best-known landmarks.

The other fascinating building on Uphill Hill is the church, which dates back to Norman times. Legend has it that the church was being built at the base of the hill, but that St. Nicholas himself decided he wanted it at the top, and kept moving the stones up the hill while the villages slept. A rather more prosaic explanation is the military value of its elevated viewpoint – or even its use by sailors as a landmark. On a stormy day it has a spectacular setting, perched on the edge of this windswept hill, overlooking the sea and large parts of Somerset.

The church is now partly ruined, unfortunately, and not in regular use (it is a bit of a stiff climb up from the village!). It was still used, though, up until Victorian times, when a new church with the same name was built down in the village in a rather more sheltered spot.

The hilltop is a bracing, windy spot which can be very invigorating in the winter. It's also a great place for kite-flying!

From the church, take the rocky track back down to the road. You are now within a stone's throw of the Ship Inn, which is facing you to the right.

The Ship Inn

There are two pubs close together in Uphill. The Dolphin is the older. It's also the smaller of the two, and by comparison with the Ship, a bit dingy. The Ship, on the other hand, has been recently refurbished, and has a novel three-level design. The public bar is on the ground floor, there's a children's area in the basement and the lounge area is a raised section to the left of the bar, on the stairs leading up to the (generously-sized) dining area.

The Ship Inn, Uphill. A comfortable, good value pub where you can take kids.

The bar food menu is standard pub fare – chips, scampi, steak, prawn cocktail etc. – no surprises here. Quality is fair, as are the prices. It's a Whitbread pub, and usually offers three real ales. When this book was being written, these were Marstons Pedigree, Flowers Original and

Draught Bass. Draught Bass is, in my opinion, the finest beer ever brewed. However here, as in most pubs, it's ruthlessly murdered with aeration at the pump (to give it a head) and a slightly warm cellar. Marstons Pedigree is always a safe bet, while the Flowers is as insipid as it is everywhere.

The Ship Inn is really a locals/holiday-makers pub decorated rather more tastefully than usual. It's pleasant, with decent enough food and a fair selection of beers. For a bit more local colour, try the Dolphin. Both pubs offer only roadside parking. Fortunately, there's a pretty large free car park a little way along the road to the beach.

Brean Down

Route: Brean Farm – Brean Down – abandoned fort – Fiddler's Point

Distance: 6 miles

Start: The Brean Down Inn, Brean (ST 297570)

By Car: From Weston-super-Mare, take the A370 south. Just after you've passed Uphill and before you get to Bleadon, there's a junction to the right, next to the Anchor Pub. This road twists and turns for half a mile, then follows the side of the railway line for a mile. Once over the railway bridge, look out for another right turn, about half a mile further on. After a couple of miles of twisty country driving, the road turns sharply to the right. Ignore the junction on the left. The road now leads into Brean – you join the coast road here. Turn right towards Brean Down, and you'll find the Brean Down Inn about half a mile down the road, on the right. It has a large car park to the front and side.

The Walk

Brean Down is a high, rolling peninsula which sticks out over a mile into the Bristol Channel. It reaches a height of 320 feet and is one of the most prominent landmarks along this section of coastline.

The whole down belongs to the National Trust, and the walkways are clearly visible and well maintained. (Really, there are only two – the broad, grassy walk along the ridge and the metalled track running along the northern slopes.)

As with the rest of the Mendips, Brean Down has been inhabited since Roman times. There's evidence of the existence of a Roman temple here, and an Iron Age settlement. More recently, fortifications were built at the western tip at the time of the Napoleonic Wars, and added to during World War Two. These buildings are now derelict, but they are still standing and are a fascinating relic in a stunning location.

*Brean Down is a rolling peninsula jutting two miles out
into the Bristol Channel*

Interestingly, if Isambard Kingdom Brunel had had his way, Brean Down would now be a major sea port! He had planned to build a rail link to this isolated spot, but it never happened. (If it had, the whole commercial geography of the area would have been quite different.)

I feel the walk from the Brean Down Inn, along Brean Down and then back again is slightly contrived because it's not a truly circular route. The Brean Down Inn, however, is the only pub in the locality – and anyway, the walk along the beach to the down is both spectacular and bracing!

From the Brean Down Inn, you'll see a footpath leading between the dunes down on to the beach (on the opposite side of the road and slightly to the left). You now emerge on an amazing seven-mile stretch of beach that starts at Brean Down to the north and ends at the coastal town of Burnham-on-Sea, near Highbridge. The beach is flat, wide and exposed. In spring and autumn (and winter!) the wind can be strong and biting. The Victorians used to believe this stretch of coastline (especially

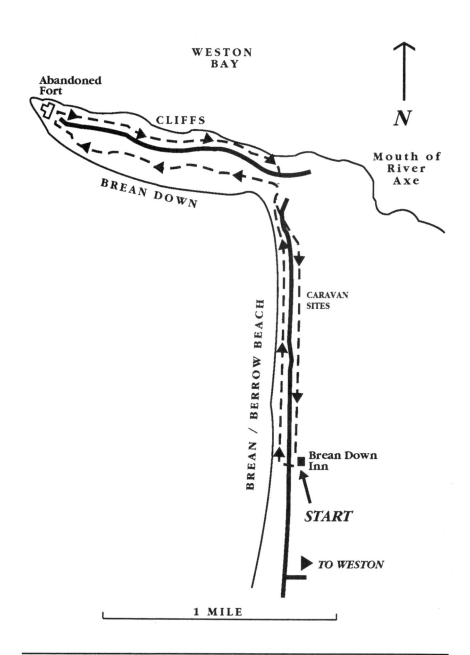

the sands at Weston-super-Mare) was healthy and 'bracing', which explains the rapid expansion of the region's seaside resorts in the nineteenth century.

Once on the beach, head north towards Brean Down. If you don't want to park your car outside the pub, you can drive it down on to the beach. But you have to pay for the privilege in the summer – and you have to watch the tide, too. This coastline has one of the highest tidal ranges in the world. The substantial sea defences all along this coast are not just for show.

As you reach the base of the down, you'll see a group of shops ahead. Climb the slipway at this point, then head past the shops to climb the path up on to the down – it's clearly visible from some distance away.

I haven't counted the steps on the way up to the top, but there are lots. If you don't stop to catch your breath at least twice you're either superhuman or taking it very easy indeed. Once at the top of the steps, the whole of Weston bay comes into view. And if you turn around, you can see right along the coastline towards Burnham-on-Sea and beyond. In the right conditions, the Quantock Hills and Exmoor are clearly visible. You'll also see a broad, grassy track heading off to the left and out to sea. This is the route you want to follow.

The walk along the down is one of the most spectacular upland routes anywhere – not bad for a ridge that barely rises above 300 feet. Ahead, the twin islands of Steepholm and Flatholm are more clearly visible than from any other vantage point, and beyond them, the coast of South Wales can be incredibly clear (and the hills inland, too). This walk is exposed, though, so you can expect to feel the full force of the weather. On a good day you'll be invigorated, on a bad day you'll wish you hadn't left your muffler in the car.

There are two high points to climb, neither very demanding. It's only as you crest the second (highest) summit that the abandoned fort at the tip of the headland comes into view far below.

Despite intermittent restoration work, the fort has never been much of tourist attraction. Part of the reason is its isolation – it can only be reached by foot, and even then only from a place well off the beaten track. It's also not very well-known, except amongst the locals. Those who do know it, though, go back again and again to absorb its eerie atmosphere and spectacular location. The buildings are principally nineteenth century, but many concrete fortifications were added just before the Second World War, including gun platforms and concrete blockhouses.

The route back is easier. A metalled track (now breaking up, but still serviceable) runs along the northern edge of Brean Down. From here you can take in the panoramic views across Weston Bay. The path gradually rises, finally meeting up with the top route more or less at the top of the steps you climbed earlier. From here, it's a straightforward walk along the road back to the pub.

During the winter, Brean is a desolate, windswept ghost town. The huge caravan sites lining the dunes are empty and locked. It's a lonely, but fascinating place. During the summer it's neither lonely *nor* fascinating! While you're not dodging cars, edging past other pedestrians and being regaled by the aroma of warm chips and sticky candy floss, though, you can still take in the views across the Axe estuary to your left. Uphill Hill and the quarry seem only a stone's throw away. As the crow flies, the distance is barely a mile. However, to reach Uphill involves a six-mile trip along twisting country roads. There is no bridge across the mouth of the Axe, and crossing it on foot or by any other means is quite impossible. During the summer there is a modest ferry service which you might like to sample; I haven't.

The Brean Down Inn

The Brean Down Inn is a large, detached pub set a little way back from the road in a large gravel car park. Alongside, there's an even larger grassy playing area for kids, complete with swings, climbing frames and so on. This pub is situated next to the sea front at Brean and in amongst dozens of medium to large caravan parks. As you might expect, then, it's very much a traditional 'holiday' pub. You can usually take this to mean beer, chips and jukeboxes. The Brean Down Inn is better than most, though.

Once in the main entrance you can go either to the right, and the Lounge Bar or ahead/to the left and the Saloon Bar. The Lounge Bar is much quieter and smaller than the Saloon, and laid out more for eating than drinking. It's not exactly the Savoy, but it's comfortable enough.

The Brean Down Inn. A spacious 'holidaymakers' pub, with more character than most.

The Saloon is more rough and ready, but a bit more lively too. It's quite large, and you shouldn't have trouble getting a seat except at the busiest times. It's quite a decent, down to earth pub.

Real ale choice on our visit was limited to Marstons Pedigree, but this is a pretty decent pint, so there are no complaints on that score. The food menu is pretty basic pub stuff, but very extensive. There are a handful of starters (soup, prawn cocktail etc) and main courses such as plaice and chips, chicken and chips and steak. With chips, that is. Non-chip fans can go for a range of salads, ploughman's, rolls and jacket spuds. There's also a separate kids menu. In addition, the Brean Down Inn specialises in home-made pizzas – about six different varieties in two different sizes.

The Brean Down Inn isn't the sort of place you'd take your mother-in-law for an evening out, but it's a decent enough holiday pub and it's also within striking distance of one of the most impressive walks on the Mendips.

Weston Woods

Route: Sand Bay – Weston Woods – Worlebury Camp – Toll Road

Distance: 4 miles

Start: The Commodore, Sand Bay (ST 329633)

By car: From Weston-super-Mare, take the coast road north, round Marine Lake, past Birnbeck Pier and then head east along the Toll Road (you have to pay a small sum during the tourist season). Turn sharp left at the end of the Toll Road and head downhill. The Commodore is on the right-hand side at the bottom of the hill.

The Walk

Considering they're right alongside a major tourist resort, Weston Woods cover a surprisingly large and unspoilt area. They're liberally criss-crossed with broad tracks and paths and, although it's not difficult to get lost or go round in circles, there are plenty of signposts to help you stay on course.

The Woods are entirely deciduous, which makes a pleasant change from the rather gloomy coniferous tracts further inland on the Mendips. Another attraction is the site of Worlebury Camp, a hill fort dating back to 300BC. Now marked only by a clearing and heaps of broken stones, the fort was probably the best-defended on the Mendips in its time.

There are a few climbs on this route, but nothing too stiff. Children and 'mature' adults should have no problems. The Toll Road can get a bit busy during the summer, though, so you may want to head back through the woods, rather than taking the coastal route on the way back.

From the Commodore, you need to head left and up the hill. After two or three hundred yards you emerge on the main Kewstoke road. Opposite, and slightly to the right, you'll see a broad track leading uphill and into the woods.

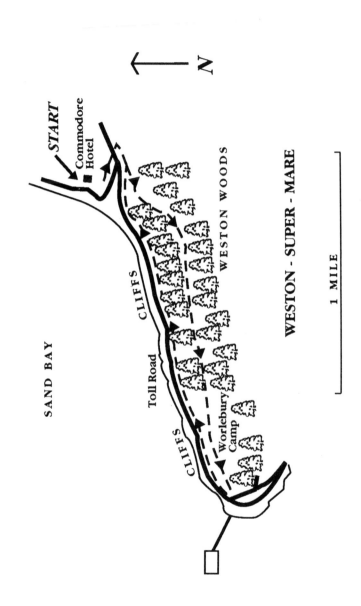

You carry on climbing as you head up this track. It's not terribly demanding, though, and within about a quarter of a mile you've arrived at a large clearing in the centre of the woods. There's parking space here, and a broad, stony road leading in from Worlebury to the east, so you could drive in if you wanted to.

When you reach this clearing, turn right. You're now on another broad track, one that leads west through the woods and towards Worlebury Camp. This is one of the few woodland walks in the Mendips that doesn't turn into a quagmire after rain. You're heading gently downhill all the time, but if you're still puffing after the climb up from the pub (shame on you!) then there are wooden benches at intervals alongside the track.

This track passes straight through the centre of Worlebury Camp, then back in amongst the trees. From here it descends towards the western end of the Woods and Birnbeck Island, ending in a flight of steps leading down to a road. You go left here, walking downhill still until you come to a T-Junction at the end. You go right here, and walk about fifty yards down to a main road and – opposite – some ornamental gardens.

From here you get excellent views of Brean Down, Steep Holm, Flat Holm and Birnbeck Pier. Go right at the fountain, through the gardens then down the steps to the road opposite Birnbeck Pier. Head right here, up the hill. Within a few yards you reach a T-junction. Go left here to follow the Toll Road along the northern edge of the Woods. (There's no toll for pedestrians!)

The Toll Road can carry quite a lot of traffic during the holiday season, and does not have any footpaths/pavements. There is an alternative, though. As you head downhill towards the toll booth, on the right you'll see a track forking off right and uphill into the Woods. You can take this track and walk back to the Commodore through the Woods again if you wish.

From the Toll Road you do get excellent views across Sand Bay towards Sand Point. From here, it looks a rather low, unimpressive finger of land, belying the rather spectacular little landscapes on the northern side. You should also be able to make out Woodspring Priory.

The Toll Road, Kewstoke. From here you get excellent views across Sand Bay.

The walk along the Toll Road gives lots of little glimpses of Sand Bay through the trees. Here and there you may find little tracks leading through the trees and out onto the cliffs. Be careful – the cliffs aren't high, but are still dangerous. The more sure-footed will be able to pick their way down to some of the isolated little coves below the trees. These are generally quiet, being used only by fishermen.

The Toll Road winds its way along the top of the cliffs for the best part of a mile and a half. There are one or two little grassy slopes above the cliffs which are ideal for picnics or breathers, while to your right as you walk are densely-wooded and steep slopes. Further on, though, there are clearings, even places to park a car.

Eventually, the Toll Road rejoins the road leading uphill from the Commodore. To save a few yards, though, you can take a short-cut here. As the Toll Road starts heading uphill at the end, look out for some steps on your left and a track running downhill through the trees. This brings you out into the public car park opposite the Commodore and next to the beach.

The Commodore

There are two pubs at Sand Bay. The Long John Silver is a cheap and cheerful holiday pub half way along the sea front. This is the most convenient for walkers on Sand Point. The Commodore, by contrast, is a fairly posh 'eating-out pub'. (There's a decent restaurant too, by the way, and accommodation is available.) The Commodore nestles at the base of Worlebury Woods, right at the Weston-super-Mare end of the sea front. It's actually built on the site of four fishermen's cottages built in the seventeenth century, although the current building appears quite new. It's named after Commodore Henry Ware.

Inside, things are a bit gloomy, but the place is nicely decorated, and there's room for perhaps three dozen pub lunchers. Beyond the eating area is the main bar, which is smaller but still a reasonable size. The bar itself is only about six feet wide, though (why?), so getting served can be a problem!

The Commodore Hotel, Sand Bay. A good place to eat, either from the carvery or in the restaurant.

The beer choice consists of Butcombe (a local brew – a bit variable in my experience, but lots like it), Flowers (nothing to write home about) and draught Bass (great).

The food here is well above average. There are half a dozen starters to choose from and a whole host of main courses, including things like 'Steak and Bake' and 'Pan-Fried Darne of Salmon'. There's a daily carvery-style roast and traditional beef lunches on Sundays. On top of that there are various vegetarian dishes, salads and snacks. Best of all, the prices are very reasonable.

Kids are not especially well catered for. Over-14s can go in the bars but that's about it. However, there is a good play area next to the car park, with swings, climbing equipment and tables and benches.

Car parking isn't a problem. The pub itself has a huge gravel car park to the rear, while there's a smaller public car park just over the road. The site makes the Commodore a great base for exploring Worlebury Woods (and the British Camp towards the Birnbeck Island end), and the Woods' broad, clear paths make it an easy place for youngsters and old folk alike.

Sand Point

Route: Sand Bay – Sand Point – Middle Hope

Distance: 7 miles

Start: The Long John Silver, Sand Bay (ST 332646)

By car: From Weston-super-Mare sea front, head north, following the road as it passes Knightstone, curves round Madeira Cove and heads uphill, passing the Old Pier (Birnbeck Island). Just here it joins the Toll Road which runs along the northern slopes of Worlebury Woods. You will have to pay a small toll during the holiday season. At the end of the Toll Road, a sharp turn left takes you down into Sand Bay and on to the road running parallel with the sea wall. The Long John Silver is a little more than half a mile along this road, on the right. It has its own, large, car park, and there is some roadside parking outside.

The Walk

Sand Point is uncannily like Brean Down. It's another slim finger of land poking out into the Bristol Channel, and another National Trust Site. And, like the Brean Down walk, this one starts from a pub on the sea front. Again, it's not ideal, but it's the only pub within striking distance. And no walking guide to the Mendips would be complete without a description of Sand Point.

Although Sand Point is very much like Brean Down, it's a great deal smaller. While Brean Down is a great hulking mass, Sand Point is a far more modest little peninsula which rises to no more than half the height and is only half the length.

However, it does include some superb cliff-top walking, excellent sea views, varied landscape and even quite a lot of historical interest. Part of this is provided by the remains of a Celtic field system around the surprisingly steep northern slopes of the hills at Middle Hope. The main

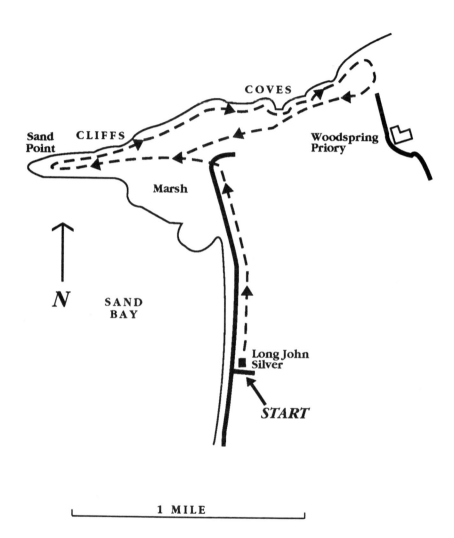

COVES

Sand
Point

CLIFFS

Woodspring
Priory

Marsh

↑

N   SAND
         BAY

Long John
Silver

START

1 MILE

Sand Point offers some excellent coastal walking, well off the beaten track.

attraction, though is Woodspring Priory, near the eastern end of the National Trust reserve. The Priory was founded at the start of the thirteenth century (before that there was a chapel here). It was dedicated to St. Thomas à Becket after his murder in Canterbury Cathedral in 1170. There must have been a collective feeling of guilt locally, because one of the killers lived here. The martyr's blood was collected in four wooden cups, one of which came to Woodspring Priory. Then, during the infamous dissolution of the monasteries, the cup was removed to Kewstoke church for safety. And in 1849, a cup was discovered during renovations that experts believe is one of those containing the blood of Thomas à Becket. It is now kept at Taunton museum.

Now the annoying thing is, that it's only a short walk down to the Priory from the National Trust reserve, but this walk is along a private road; so if you want to visit the Priory, rather than just admire it from nearby, you'll have to drive round from the other side.

Starting from the Long John Silver, you can either walk along the beach or the road to Sand Point. Unlike the beach at Brean, Sand Bay beach is distinctly unspectacular. Even during the summer, the place is hardly a tourist mecca, and the general air is one of disuse and decay.

Disuse or not, the military obviously thought the bay had strategic importance. There are concrete pillboxes hidden amongst the dunes, even one at the edge of the beach, tilted and half-buried in the sand.

At the northern end of the beach, as you near Sand Point, the sand gives way to a marshy, boggy area invaded regularly by the tide. At this point, if you haven't yet rejoined the road, I'd recommend it. There is, incidentally, a car park at the base of Sand Point, but you'll have to pay for the privilege of using it.

From the car park, there's a clear path upwards and to the left, taking you out on to the top of the ridge. Once at the top (there's a triangulation pillar here) you are only 160 feet above sea level, but you still get superb views of the sea and the surrounding countryside. To the south is the sweep of Sand Bay, with the dark mass of Worlebury Woods on the other side. You can also see Birnbeck Pier, that relic of Victorian seaside architecture, and beyond that Brean Down. To the west are the islands of Steep Holm and Flat Holm, and beyond those the coast of South Wales, bearing round to the north.

Follow the path west now, and out to sea. Further on, the path gets narrower, steeper and quite rocky. You have to watch your step here – you could quite easily twist an ankle. Sand Point ends with jagged rocks sloping down into the sea. After pausing to take in the dramatic coastline of Wales across the sea, turn round and pick up the lower path along the northern slopes. This follows the low cliffs at the edge of the sea. Be careful again here. These paths are not used much and they're narrow and slippery. The cliffs aren't high enough to give you vertigo, but quite high enough to give you broken bones – or worse.

This path takes in some beautiful coastal scenery. On the left are many tiny, secluded coves, while the rolling hills to your right are surprisingly steep. After about a mile, you'll have to cut uphill to a stile in a stone wall. Once over this you can head back down to the sea to take in the last (and best!) half mile or so of coastline before heading directly uphill and then back along the top of the ridge, following the boundary of the reserve (the land to the east of the reserve is owned by the MOD, while that to the south is private farmland). To the south at this point you can now see Woodspring Priory and its surrounding hamlet. Unfortunately, the metalled track leading down into it is marked as private.

Law-abiding walkers must now head back to the path leading down to the car park and the road along the sea front, leaving Woodspring Priory for another day.

The Long John Silver

This pub has a bit of a piratical theme about it, and certainly it's in the right spot. The Somerset beaches were a favourite landing point for smugglers trying to dodge the excise men, and the beach at Sand Bay is a quiet, isolated spot...

Not that you're likely to see many smugglers these days. In fact, by far the majority of the people walking the beach or sampling the hospitality at The Long John Silver will be holiday-makers. Sand Bay is nowhere near as popular as neighbouring Weston-super-Mare, but still sports a Pontin's holiday camp and numerous caravan parks.

Predictably, then, The Long John Silver is a typical 'holiday pub' – cheap and cheerful, in other words. The main bar is upstairs (The Crows Nest

The Long John Silver, Sand Bay. A pub with a piratical theme! Cheap and cheerful, but excellent value.

Bar). You can order food here, and sit at the windows looking out over the sea towards Wales. Downstairs is the 'Lower Deck Bar', which is more rough and ready. There's a games room here, with a pool table and video games machines to keep the kids occupied.

The beer choice is pretty good. Most holiday pubs specialise in anonymous and unpleasant keg beers, but the Long John Silver also sells Bass (hurrah!), Wadworths' 6X (good) and Henry's IPA, which is distinctly weedy.

The food menu is pretty predictable stuff – cod & chips, pie & chips, ploughman's lunch, jacket potatoes etc. It's notable in one respect, though – it's just about the cheapest pub food around.

If the weather's fine and you don't fancy being cooped up indoors, there are tables outside, next to the road. It's a long way from being a 'garden', though, so don't expect too much.

Parking is good, thanks to a large parking area to the side of the pub. There are also a couple of spaces outside on the road. There's also a public car park a little way along the sea front in the Weston-super-Mare direction.

Hutton

Route: Hutton – Hay Wood – Hutton Hill – Canada Combe

Distance: 3 miles

Start: The Old Inn, Hutton (ST 350587)

By car: Take the A370 south out of Weston-super-Mare then, at the major roundabout by the hospital on the outskirts, turn left. Hutton village is about two miles along this road, and the Old Inn is on the left as you drive through. The pub has a good-sized car park at the rear, and there is plenty of roadside parking in the surrounding streets.

The Walk

This walk involves a fairly stiff climb up Hutton Hill through Hay Wood, and in the summer months it can get pretty overgrown. You are rewarded, though with a delightful stroll along the top of the hill above Hutton, followed by a descent through woodland to the secluded Canada Combe.

From the Old Inn, cross the main road to head up Orchard Road. This leads you to the base of Hutton Hill. When you get there, turn left, walk along the road for a few yards and then look for a signpost at a gate on the right, indicating a public footpath up the hill. Head uphill, keeping the fence to your left. At the top of the field you'll come to a stile. Once you've climbed over, look out for a narrow track on your left. This too is signposted, although it may be a little hard to spot if the hedge hasn't been cut back recently. Don't take the broader gravel track a few feet further on – this is a dead-end.

This path leads you to another stile and another signpost. This points uphill and to the right, to the path that leads up through Hay Wood. This path starts off well enough, but soon becomes quite steep, sometimes slippery and often overgrown.

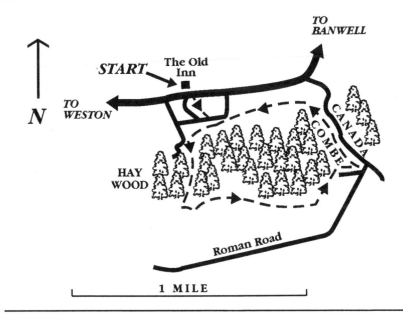

Unless you get horribly lost (unlikely) you'll arrive at another stile – you know you're on the right track now. From here, the path gets worse. It's not steep, but it's clearly not used too often and can get very overgrown.

Once you emerge from Hay Wood, look out for a stile to your left, together with an arrow showing you which way the path goes. Again, in the summer months this can get pretty overgrown. It's pretty easy to lose the route amidst a tangle of gorse and brambles. Once over this stile, you should be able to make out the track as it crosses the field beyond, but anyway, aim across the field toward the nearest corner of the wood on the other side.

Make the most of some pleasant open walking now, as you travel parallel with the 'Roman Road' which runs along the ridge of Bleadon Hill. It's thought to have once formed part of a direct link between Charterhouse, the main site for the Romans' lead-mining industry, and Uphill, the principal Mendip port of the day.

When you reach the corner of the wood you'll find another stile. Keep walking along the edge of the wood to another stile which leads you back in amongst the trees.

Roman Road, above Hutton. The fields above Hay Wood offer
excellent summer walking.

The route is very clear now. It takes you gently downhill through Hay
Wood towards Canada Combe. Bear left after the next stile. Within a
couple of hundred yards you join a gravel track which leads you down
into Canada Combe.

Follow the road downhill to the left now. After a few twists and turns –
and a distance of about 400 yards – look out for a gravel layby and a
gate to your left. There is a public footpath here which leads around the
right-hand edge of the field facing you. At the next stile, keep heading
west towards the distinctive shape of Brean Down on the horizon. After
the next stile you head between some farm buildings to a road. Keep on
heading west past the church. Before long you pass an oddly familiar
signposted footpath on your left . . . you are now back at Orchard Road
and within a short walk of the Old Inn.

The Old Inn

The Old Inn is a Tavern Fayre pub. It's recently been refurbished, and
the interior consists of a single bar but is separated by partitions into a

number of little nooks and crannies. The menu is the usual 'chips-with-everything' pub fare, but it's presented a bit more imaginatively than usual. Prices are much the same as anywhere else.

The beers on offer on our visit included Ruddles Best and Ushers Best. The Ruddles is pretty good, but the Ushers Best wouldn't put hairs on anyone's chest.

There's a livelier, brighter atmosphere than most local pubs – it's somewhere to go for a bit more 'life', where you're least likely to be mobbed by rugby teams on a night out or coachloads of pensioners on a mystery tour. It's by no means a 'traditional' pub, with ancient farmers slumped over corner tables or decrepit bulldogs draped in front of roaring fires – for that you'll have to go further inland.

If you're a bit grubby after your trek through the woods, there are tables outside. There is also generous car parking at the rear of the pub. The New Inn is a decent, modern pub which is quite tastefully managed and a fun place to be.

The Old Inn, Hutton. A 'young', vibrant pub, with a good choice of food and great atmosphere.

Around Bleadon

Route: Bleadon Village – Hellenge Hill – Combe Farm – River Axe – South Hill

Distance: 3 miles

Start: The Queen's Arms, Bleadon (ST 340570)

By car: Take the A370 south from Weston-super-Mare. A mile beyond the large roundabout and hospital at Uphill you will come to a staggered crossroads, with a turning to Brean on the right and one to Bleadon on the left. Take the left. Half a mile later the road will turn sharply to the left as you enter the village. There is a free car park almost immediately on your left, while the Queen's Arms (which has only a small car park) is just fifty yards further up the road.

The Walk

Bleadon is a fairly unremarkable-looking little village just to the south of Weston-super-Mare. It's got a rather nice old pub, however, plus some decent views and a pleasant stretch of riverside walking. What this walk lacks in length, it makes up for in variety.

The name 'Bleadon' may have come from the Celtic words 'Blai' ('wolf') and 'Don' ('hill'). Wolves once lived in and around the Mendips – a wolf den has been uncovered near Crook Peak. Or it may have come from 'Bleodun' – a word that describes the characteristic the blue/green/grey colour of limestone hills.

The favourite local legend concerns a gang of Danish raiders who sent the villagers fleeing to the hills. All but a lame woman, that is, who hid and then made her way to the Axe and set the Danes' ships adrift. The villagers took heart from this act of bravery and returned to annihilate the Danes, after which the site was called 'Bleed Down'.

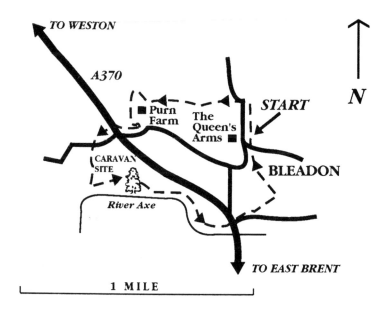

The going is generally good, but there are muddy sections – wear shoes with plenty of grip, and maybe even wellingtons if it's rained recently.

As you leave the pub, turn left to head up the hill. After about three hundred yards the road will curve sharply to the left. Look for a bus stop on the corner. Just beyond this there is a wooden marker post indicating a public footpath. Climb down the wooden ladder on the other side of the wall, and then strike out towards the corner of the wall facing you. Skirt this wall, bearing right.

To the left you'll get a good view of the curiously-shaped Brent Knoll, once used in ancient times as a hill fort – the outline of the earthworks is still visible if you climb to the top. After a short distance you'll arrive at a pair of stiles only a few yards apart. Climb over both of these, following the footpath markers (wooden posts with yellow tips).

Now head diagonally across the field, aiming for the right hand corner of a clump of trees on the other side, about a hundred yards away. Skirt round these trees, bearing to the left.

Turn right to follow the footpath past some allotments and new houses. You'll get plenty of practice climbing stiles, since there are half a dozen of the things in the space of a couple of hundred yards! The allotments here are a comparatively modern invention, but it's believed the hillside above was farmed by the Celts.

Ignore any tracks leading off to the left, and head straight on for the farm buildings visible at the base of the hill. As you draw near to a large cylindrical storage building, look out for a stile on your right and a sign indicating a public footpath. It can get a bit muddy round here, so make sure your trouser legs are tucked into your socks – and watch your footing!

Climb over the stile and skirt round the right hand side of the farm buildings. Incidentally, the farmhouse at Purn Farm was designed by Robert Adams in the late eighteenth century. He also designed Harewood House and Osterley Park, amongst other notable buildings. You now climb over another stile within a few yards – you're heading for a broad, well-defined track heading up the hill facing you. Follow the signposts carefully to make sure you stay on the correct side of the fencing.

As you head up this broad track you'll see a stile ahead and another footpath marker. Once over the stile, go right and follow the line of the hedge/trees. After about a hundred yards you'll see an overgrown stone wall ahead, and another track merging in from the left. Take this track, almost doubling back on yourself but walking along the ridge of the hill this time.

From here you get excellent views. To the south east is Bleadon village, to the south Brent Knoll. Look to the west and you will see the whale-like promontory of Brean Down and, beyond it, Steep Holm island, out in the Bristol Channel. Depending on how clear the air is, you may also be able to see the Somerset and Devon coastline way over to the south west, and maybe Glastonbury Tor on the horizon to the south east.

Nearby is a broad track heading up the hill from the main road below. The story is that if you're on the hill at midnight on the anniversary of the Battle of Sedgemoor (July 6th), you can hear the shouting and singing of soldiers returning from the battle.

From here, head back more or less the way you came, but along the ridge of the hill. It ends fairly abruptly in a steep, overgrown slope. Bear sharp left and head down to the track around the base of the hill. Turn right when you reach it and you will come to a gate leading back down to Combe Farm. Once through the gate, head straight for the road.

When you reach the road, turn right. Within a couple of hundred yards you'll reach the main road. Cross carefully, as this can get very busy! Once across the main road, go right and then down the road to the left, immediately after the Anchor pub.

River Axe, Bleadon. The Axe is a tranquil little river meandering across the Somerset flatlands.

After a hundred yards this road bears right. Don't follow it. Instead, take the broad track that leads straight on. This is another potentially muddy spot, since it's used frequently by farm vehicles. Follow this track, leaving behind the Purn Farm Caravan Park on your left, until you reach another track forking off to the left through a gateway.

You soon find out it's one of the shortest tracks in the world! Once through the gateway, the 'track' effectively disappears. Now just follow the bank of the river Axe. Within a couple of hundred yards you'll reach a clump of trees, go left to skirt round these, going through a gateway on your right when you reach the corner of the caravan park. Follow the edge of the clump of trees round to your right, which brings you back to the river bank again.

This section is very relaxing, the roar of the traffic confined to a murmur in the distance. You may catch a glimpse of swans or herons and other wildfowl, depending on whether the local anglers are out in force.

Now follow the river bank for half a mile until you reach habitation and the main road. You now need to go left for about fifty yards, then cross the road (again, be careful) to head up a minor road opposite. (The first of two turnings – the second is by a petrol station).

Follow this first road, past the houses, past a sign which says "No Through Road", and then turn left to take the signposted public footpath about fifty yard further on. Go through an iron gate then head uphill to skirt round the old quarry workings below South Hill. Keeping the fence to your left, you'll see Bleadon village church appearing over the brow of the hill. The track gets a bit steeper and muddier here. Head down between the bushes, still in the direction of the church, and you'll reach another iron gate.

Once through here you walk down a narrow footpath between houses and gardens. The footpath leads to the churchyard. The church of St. Peter and St. Paul, incidentally, dates from 1317. Walk through the churchyard then down to the road beyond. The Queen's Arms is barely a stone's throw to your right, the free car park a similar distance down the hill to your left.

The Queen's Arms

The Queen's Arms is a small and cosy pub to look at and just as small and cosy when you go inside. To your left is the 'Smoke Room' (the equivalent of a public bar). This is quite small, with two or three tables and room at the bar for no more than four people.

To the right and ahead are two lounge areas, one set out for eating, the other with more comfortable padded chairs for relaxed drinking. Both of these areas could seat a dozen and a half people at a pinch. The interior is almost, but not quite, cramped, and really very quaint. It's hard to imagine that it's changed much for decades. There are so many nooks and crannies that it's easy to find your own little corner.

The Queen's Arms, Bleadon. Tiny, cosy and with a huge selection of 'speciality' beers.

On the beer front, there's lots to choose from. On our visit, Flowers I.P.A. was being served on the bar, while there were half a dozen 'speciality' beers available from barrels behind the bar. These included such unknown delights as 'Devon Glory' and 'Old Thumper'. The mind boggles. The selection of guest beers is changed regularly.

The choice of food is less spectacular – particularly since it's only served at lunchtimes (this may have changed by the time you're reading this). There's a basic bar food menu, all at reasonable prices. Not the sort of menu you'd make a point of seeking out, but perfectly satisfying after a bracing walk.

Kids are allowed in either of the lounge areas, provided they don't approach the bar. There's a modest car park behind the pub and *some* roadside parking up the hill outside.

Introduction to the
Western Hills

The Walks

Brent Knoll From The Red Cow, Brent Knoll (ST 332508)

Banwell Hill From The Brewers Arms, Banwell (ST 399593)

Crook Peak From The White Hart, Cross (ST 416547)

Dolebury Camp From The Crown, Churchill (ST 446596)

Around Shipham From The Miners Arms, Shipham (ST 444575)

Around Axbridge From The Almshouse Tavern, Axbridge (ST 432545)

The Area

The western Mendip hills are the most rugged and spectacular part of the range. At this point they still form a quite narrow ridge across the country and rise steeply out of the surrounding flatlands.

Brent Knoll is one of the most striking local landmarks, lying like an extinct volcano in the middle of flat farmland. It was once known as the 'Isle of Frogs'. This is because it really was once an island, and not so long ago either. Until the land was drained and reclaimed during the Middle Ages, Brent Knoll could only be reached by boat. It was used as a hill fortress in the Iron Age, and the remains of the settlement can still be seen on the summit.

From the top of Brent Knoll you can easily make out the great lumbering masses of Crook Peak and Wavering Down. These offer some excellent upland walking for the fit.

Just to the north of Crook Peak is Banwell Hill. This is altogether more gentle, but features some very pleasant woodland walking and offers excellent views to the south, as well as a glimpse of 'old' Banwell.

Further east, the Mendips begin to rise towards their central plateau. High above the crossroads at Churchill looms Dolebury Camp, another Iron Age hill fort. Almost invisible from the road, this fort enjoys one of the most spectacular locations on the Mendips.

The results of more recent human activities can be seen around nearby Shipham, which has been a small-scale mining area for centuries – the scars on the landscape are now largely overgrown, though.

Meanwhile, further south, on the southern edge of the hills, in fact, is the medieval town of Axbridge. The village features some fascinating architecture and was at one time a major local commercial centre.

Brent Knoll

Route: Brent Knoll – East Brent – Brent Knoll hill fort

Distance: 4 miles

Start: The Red Cow, Brent Knoll (ST 332508)

By Car: Take the A370 south from Weston-super-Mare. Seven miles from Weston, the A38 merges in from the north west at a roundabout. Carry on straight ahead on what is now the A38. After another mile you will join a dual-carriageway. Look for a turning on your right at the base of Brent Knoll. The Red Cow is a half a mile along this road on the right hand side. It has a large car park – there is also plenty of roadside parking and another car park a quarter of a mile down the road towards the A38.

The Walk

Brent Knoll is a rather strange volcano-shaped hill rising out of the flatlands to the south of the Mendips to a height of 450ft. On the summit are the remains of an Iron Age hill fort, where the Saxons held out against marauding Danish invaders (King Alfred fought the Danes at nearby Battleborough).

Centuries ago the Somerset Levels were more or less permanently flooded, and Brent Knoll was in fact an island which had to be reached by boat! (It was known as the Isle of Frogs.) Extensive drainage and reclamation work throughout the centuries has turned marshland into farmland, though, and sea defences along the coast prevent any further flooding.

Although Brent Knoll doesn't form part of the main body of the Mendips as such, I still think of it as part of the range. It gives you an excellent view of the sweep of the Mendips to the north, together with (on the right day) glimpses of the Quantocks and Exmoor across the sea

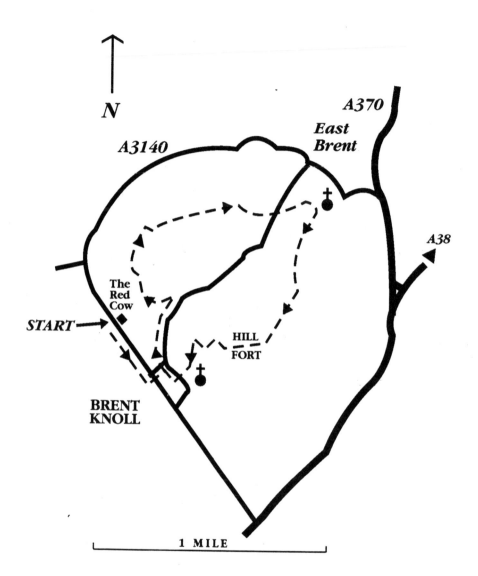

to the south west.

There are a couple of stiff little climbs on this walk, but nothing too taxing. The going is generally good, but there's enough mud to make proper walking boots (or wellingtons) essential. There are also dozens (at least it feels like dozens!) of stiles, so you'll need to be feeling pretty supple.

Depending on whether you're starting from the Red Cow itself, or the car park nearer the A38, head left or right respectively along the road. After a quarter of a mile (that's from the Red Cow – it's far less from the car park), you'll see a road marked 'Church Road' leading up to the base of the hill. Follow this for 150 yards and you'll reach a fork with a signpost. Follow the route signposted 'To the Knoll'.

This road curves to the right, steepening. After 400 yards you come to a crossroads. Ahead of you the road carries on over the knoll. To your right is track leading up to the top of the knoll. To your left is a large, grassy car park. Go left.

This bit can be a bit tricky because there are paths either side of the car park. Both lead to private buildings. Instead of taking these, walk through the car park (about 100 yards) until it opens out into a larger field. Ahead of you across the field is a private house. Follow the fence on the left of the field, heading round to the right, and you will see a white-painted stile about 200 yards away across the field. This is the route you want to take.

Brent Knoll is a major landmark for miles around. It's visible from the southern edge of the Mendips for most of their length. The knoll itself is at the southern end of a larger plateau about a mile across. Our route follows the rim of this plateau, and gives you views not only of the knoll but the seaside towns of Berrow and Brean and the Bristol Channel too. You can see the lumbering hulk of Brean Down near Weston-super-Mare and, beyond that, the two islands of Steep Holm and Flat Holm. On a clear day you will also be able to make out the coastal towns and rising mountains of South Wales.

The path is reasonably clearly defined from here. Keep looking out for stiles and you won't go wrong. With the house about a third of a mile behind you you'll come to a fenced-off site apparently blocking your path. Don't worry – there's a stile in the left-hand corner of this field and a fenced-off path around the site. When you emerge, head directly towards the knoll for about 50 yards then look for a stile into the field on your left. Once over this stile, you should be able to make out the spire of the church at East Brent nestling at the base of the hill. Head for this across the field and you should soon see another stile in the hedge ahead of you. There's a good rule of thumb for this walk; if you see a stile, you're supposed to go over it!

Climb over the next stile and you'll be confronted with a wooded and apparently impassable dip between you and the church. Don't worry! Head downwards to the right and, right at the base of the dip, you'll find a decidedly rustic bridge across a stream. The climb up the other side can be a bit fraught because it's short but steep, and usually very muddy. Thankfully, there are trees to grab hold of.

After a short climb you'll emerge out into the open again. Walk with the hedge on your left for about 200 yards and you'll come to a road. Turn left and, very shortly, you'll see a stile on the right hand side. Climb over this and then descend to East Brent church.

Once in the churchyard, don't be tempted to follow the footpath leading off to the right. Instead, walk around to the front of the church. You'll see a reasonably-sized car park over to your right. From here the route to the top of the knoll is signposted.

This is the only real climb of the walk, and even this isn't particularly severe. You walk up a gradually steepening ridge which is only taxing for the last 200 yards or so.

And the climb is well worth it, because on a clear day the views from the top of Brent Knoll can be breathtaking. The hill affords you a full 360-degree panorama of the surrounding countryside. To the north is Weston-super-Mare and the start of the Mendip range. Turn slowly clockwise and you'll be able to follow the line of the Mendips over the rolling hills above Bleadon to the great gash in the hills where the M5 motorway streams through. To the right of this is the instantly-recognisable hooked shape of Crook Peak and to the right of that the sweeping moorland of Wavering Down and Fry's Hill. Further to the

Brent Knoll is an iron-age hill fort and a prominent landmark for miles around.

right, almost due East, you should be able to make out the deep slash of Cheddar Gorge.

The hilltop itself consists of a circular rim surrounding a shallow depression. In an age where wars are fought across entire countries, the size of the Brent Knoll hill fort makes you realise how tiny and localised conflicts were in the past.

Walk clockwise a little way around this rim and you can see the mystical Glastonbury Tor (one of the many sites claiming to be the home of King Arthur and Camelot) over in the distance to the south-east. You're now looking across the valley of the river Brue. Historically this was 'Brent Marsh', but Arthurian legend has taken over and this is now known generally as the Vale of Avalon.

To the right (south) you should be able to make out the low Polden Hills, the site of the infamous Battle of Sedgemoor of 1685.

Carry on round the rim of the hill fort and you'll see the town of Burnham-on-Sea and its distinctive white lighthouse to the west. The lighthouse, now swallowed up by housing developments, was occupied by a lighthouse keeper and assistant until 1970. Now, though, it's fully automated and is unmanned.

Beyond that is the mouth of the Parrett (the longest river in Somerset) and the Steart Island bird sanctuary. You should also be able to see Hinkley Point nuclear power station.

In the best of weather Brent Knoll also provides an excellent view of the Somerset Quantock hills and even Exmoor over to the south west. You might even be able to make out Foreland Point above Lynmouth in North Devon.

Once you've had a rest, and taken in the excellent views, carry on round the rim of the knoll, past a triangulation pillar, until you come to a path leading downwards (the first few yards consist of steps). Follow this path down the hill – you're aiming in the general direction of Brent Knoll church spire. As you near the church (about 400 yards from the top of the knoll) look out for an iron gate in the hedge to your left. This leads on to a path which takes you around the back of the church to the churchyard. When you emerge from the churchyard, go right. When you come to the main road running through East Brent, turn left for the smaller car park (about 100 yards) or right for the Red Cow (about 400 yards).

The Red Cow

The Red Cow is a Whitbread pub nestling below Brent Knoll on the main street running through the village of East Brent. Although it's in a farming area, East Brent is a fairly well-to-do little place, so the Red Cow is by no means a spit-and-sawdust pub.

In fact, it's a good spot for a meal out. The lounge bar is nicely decorated, large enough to set two or three dozen without overcrowding, and offers a decent pub menu including such staples as sirloin steak, lasagne verdi, ploughman's lunches and the various other dishes that any self-respecting pub offers. The menu may boast, however, such exotica as grilled catfish, goujons of salmon or duck breast in orange sauce... all in all, a decent venue for an evening out. Prices are about average for pub food, but the quality a little higher than usual.

The Red Cow, Brent Knoll. An excellent bar menu for those special evenings out.

However, if you've just returned from a (possibly muddy) hike around Brent Knoll, the public bar is a better bet. The decor is basic, but clean and tidy, and there's a small dining/children's area off to one side.

There's usually a small selection of draught beers on offer – for example, Boddingtons, Flowers IPA and Marstons Pedigree. Boddingtons is arguably the most interesting, with a pale colour and quite delicate flavour. Flowers IPA is pretty weak, while Pedigree is a solid, strong-flavoured bitter.

The Red Cow also has a garden and a very decent-sized car park. It's pleasant, reasonably-priced, easy to get to and easy to park at... yet it's also off the usual tourist track. What more could you ask for?

Banwell Hill

Route: Banwell – Banwell Hill – The Caves – Knightcott

Distance: 3.5 miles

Start: The Brewers Arms, Banwell (ST 399593)

By Car: From Weston-super-Mare, take the A371, heading east. Head through Banwell village until the point where the road curves sharply right to head uphill towards Banwell castle. Look out for a small left turning approximately 50-100 yards after this curve in the road. (There is a major turning to the left a few yards further on – don't take this one by mistake). This narrow road leads downhill past St. Andrews church, curving to the left. The Brewers Arms is about 200 yards beyond the church, on the left hand side of the road. There's a modest-sized car park to the rear and some roadside parking.

The Walk

Banwell is a mixture of old and new. The new comes in the form of modern housing developments to the west along the A371 as it descends into the village, and the sheer volume of traffic that passes through the village – especially heavily-laden lorries travelling to and from the many quarries on the Mendips. The village's main street really isn't up to the quantity of traffic passing through, and this tends to detract from Banwell's appeal.

Which is a pity, because once you get away from the main road, you find it's a charming little place. If you go back far enough it becomes apparent the village was really in two separate halves – 'lowland' and 'upland'. The lowland parts (including the site of the Brewers Arms) are largely below sea level, while the upper village (mainly following High Street) is on the slopes of Banwell Hill.

At the top of the road leading south out of Banwell (the A371) is Banwell Castle. It looks in pretty good shape for a medieval ruin, until you learn that it was in fact built in the nineteenth century. Any further plans for exploration are scotched by the fact that it still is a private residence, and is not open to the public (although it currently houses a tea shop).

This walk takes you through the busy little village of Banwell then up on to Banwell Hill. The walk around the hill gives excellent views across towards the distinctive Crook Peak and Wavering Down. It's an excellent walk for 'getting away from it all' despite its comparatively short length.

For the most part the going is easy, but there is one short climb near the start, and the going near The Caves can get pretty muddy. Boots are recommended, although ordinary footwear will be all right in dry weather.

When you leave the Brewers Arms, walk up the road towards St. Andrews church. You'll pass a neatly-maintained bowling green on your right. Shortly the road curves round to the right, and within another hundred yards you reach the main road. Take care crossing it! You are near a main junction, between the A368 and A371, and you'll have traffic coming at you from three directions.

Cross over this road and head up the narrow road facing you. This is High Street. It takes you sharply uphill, past the car park of The Ship Inn, after which it levels off. You're now walking through an older part of the village. The narrow road is lined with small houses and cottages, and the roar of the traffic is soon left behind.

After about a hundred yards you'll see a lane forking off upwards and to the left. At the same place you'll see a narrower lane – Rocky Lane – also on the left and leading directly uphill. Both will take you up on to Banwell Hill, but be warned – Rocky Lane is aptly named! It looks very picturesque, leading up between picturesque cottages and flower gardens, but soon degenerates into a steep, rocky and slippery climb through often overgrown vegetation. Instead, take the broader lane – this too degenerates soon into a narrower, muddier path, but the going is much easier.

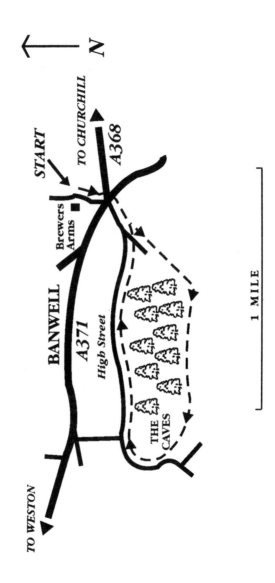

Banwell is a picturesque rural village once you're away from the main road.

Within two hundred yards you emerge from amongst the trees. Keep to the path as it curves round to the left, following the hedgerow, and you will see a gate ahead of you. Once through the gate, head for two trees standing in the middle of the field beyond. And from here, look out for another gate ahead of you, across the field. See it? Well don't aim straight for it but, instead, walk slightly to the right. As you reach the hedgerow, look out for a poorly-defined track running alongside it, heading off to the right. Follow this track – it soon becomes more definite, and the going underfoot changes from mud and grass to a gravel track.

This track now takes you around the southern edge of Banwell Hill. On a clear day you get excellent views to the south of Bleadon Hill, Crook Peak and Wavering Down. This track continues for a little over half a mile before descending to The Caves. Here there is a large, working farm and the track takes you between the farm buildings. It can get quite muddy here! Good footwear is useful not just for keeping your feet dry, but making sure you keep your footing too. In drier weather it's unlikely to be much of a problem, but in wet weather you really will need proper walking boots.

After passing through The Caves you emerge on to a narrow country road. Turn right here and follow the road as it heads downhill. After a couple of sharp turns you'll see a turning to the right. This is High Street again (look out for a sign on the right hand side). Following this road takes you back in to Banwell, a distance of about a mile. This route avoids the busy main roads and takes you through some of 'old' Banwell. When you come to the main road, simply retrace your steps back to the Brewers Arms.

The Brewers Arms

The Brewers Arms has one of the most attractive locations of any of the pubs on the Mendips. It's stands shaded by trees alongside a burbling little river, at the bottom of an old village street – an idyllic rural scene! The garden is large, overlooks the stream and features swings for the

The Brewers Arms, Banwell. A superb little garden for those warm summer evenings.

kids (there's another, smaller garden on the other side of the building). It's a perfect 'summer evening' pub.

Inside, though, it's a tiny bit less perfect. The Brewers Arms is something of a cheap 'n' cheerful 'locals' pub, albeit a comfortable and nicely decorated one. It consists of one, medium-sized room (no separate lounge and public bars) with a dividing wall in the middle. There's also a big log-effect gas fire for those chilly winter days. It can get pretty busy at times. Banwell is now a bustling community – post-war housing developments have, for better or worse, swelled the village population dramatically.

The Brewers Arms is an Ushers pub, and offers Ushers Best and Founders on draught. Ushers Best is fine for the timid, while Founders is a rather good, heavy beer and much the better of the two.

The food menu offers a good range of typical pub fare, and at pretty reasonable prices. There's also a good kids' menu – 'well-behaved' children are indeed allowed inside (but only in one area of the bar).

Crook Peak

Route: Cross – Compton Bishop – Crook Peak – Wavering Down – King's Wood

Distance: 7 miles

Start: The White Hart, Cross (ST 416547)

By car: Take the A371 out of Weston-super-Mare, through Locking and Banwell to Winscombe. Turn right here as you join the A38 and head south past Sidcot and down Shute Shelve hill. Take the right turn at the crossroads at the base of the hill and you'll find the White Hart on the right in about 200 yards. There is a fair-sized car park facing the pub, together with some roadside parking.

The Walk

This route is for more determined walkers only. It's not just the hills (although there are enough of those, and when you least feel like them!) but navigation through the early stages can be tricky too. You may find one or two of the stiles obstructed, but not impassable and there are short sections where you will have to rely on dead reckoning rather than signposting.

The effort is worth it, though, because this walk takes in some of the finest upland walking in the Mendips. Crook Peak itself offers a 360-degree panorama of the surrounding countryside. At 620 feet, it isn't the highest point on the walk – Wavering Down is a little higher at 690 feet – but it does offer the best views for miles around. It's also one of the wildest points on the Mendips. You're not too far from civilisation, but the winds up on the peak can be very strong and very cold. You're also near the site of an ancient wolf den, evidence that the area was once a bit too wild for comfort!

From the White Hart, follow the road west, looking out, in about 200 yards, for a gateway on the right hand side of the road and a footpath leading gently uphill.

This footpath leads shortly to a small, disused quarry. Walk around the left hand edge of the quarry and then through the gate that comes into view on your left about a quarter of the way round. (For the next mile, remember that you are aiming for the landmark of Crook Peak.) Once through this gate, aim ahead and slightly to the right. You will round the corner of a hedge and see a stile in the corner of the field.

From here, aim for the farm buildings visible ahead, keeping the hedge to your left. You go through another gate, then cross a patch of open ground in front of the farm buildings. Just on the other side of the buildings you'll find a gate opening on to a track leading uphill across your path. Cross this track, climbing over another stile almost directly opposite, then follow the line of the telegraph poles in the next field, walking to the right of the hedge when you reach it. At the end of this field you'll come across a rather curt notice pointing you uphill. The stile you want is hidden just a few yards away, round the corner of the hedge.

Once over this stile, carry on walking in the direction of Crook Peak. You'll come across another notice directing you uphill and around the corner . . .

Again, head towards Crook Peak. Before long, the church in Compton Bishop will become visible – this is an even better landmark to aim for. The route here is pretty vague – keep on walking with the hedgerow to your left and in the right general direction. Pretty soon the church will be in clear view, and you can't go too far wrong from here. The path veers slightly to the right of the church towards the peak again. You soon join a track leading down into Compton Bishop, leaving all your navigation worries behind you for the rest of the walk.

Compton Bishop is an odd little place lying deep within the encircling hills and rather off the beaten track. As a settlement it goes back many centuries – it used to be known as 'Compton Episcopi', and the church dates back to 1236.

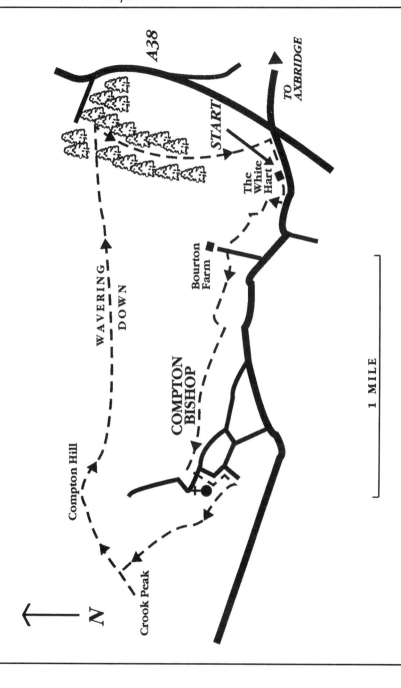

When the track emerges on to a road, turn right. Almost immediately you're at a T-junction, where you go left. This road takes you past the church. After a hundred yards start looking for a turn-off to the right (a No Through Road). This is Vicarage Lane, and within a hundred yards it turns into a stony track leading uphill between some trees. Once through a gate you reach a T-junction of footpaths. You want to take the right-hand route.

The path now winds, gently at first, up the side of Compton Hill. It gets progressively steeper, though, and the trees begin to thin out, until at last you emerge on the ridge between the rocky outcrop of Crook Peak on your left and the rolling mass of Wavering Down on your right.

There are five caves in the ridge leading up to Crook Peak from Compton Bishop, although you'd be hard pushed to find them. One – Denny's Hole – is named after St. Dennis. It was used by the Home Guard in World War Two.

Once you reach the top of the ridge, Crook Peak is a bit of a detour off

Crook Peak is one of the highlights of the Western Mendips, commanding panoramic views.

to the left. But it's well worth the few minutes it takes to get to the top. The views (and the perennial gusting winds, for that matter) are breathtaking. In ancient times it was one of the region's many beacon sites – the idea was that in the event of an invasion, a huge bonfire would be lit which would be visible many miles away. As far away as the next beacon site, in fact. In this way, warnings could be transmitted rapidly across large distances.

These days, Crook Peak is used principally by model glider enthusiasts. Some of these models are several feet across and can easily be mistaken for the real thing.

From Crook Peak, the route east along Compton Hill and Wavering Down is very clearly defined. The scale is deceptive, and what looks like a breeze of a walk is actually a fair old slog, particularly as you climb to the top of Wavering Down. On the descent down the other side you pass Hill Farm on your left. This farm looks modern enough but dates right back to Saxon times.

From here it remains downhill all the way. The path descends finally into King's Wood. This was used as a royal hunting ground even before the Norman invasion. Wild deer and boar were hunted here in medieval times too.

Once you're a hundred yards inside the wood, start looking out for a narrower footpath leading off to the right. This takes you downhill (south) through a long tongue of woodland for half a mile. When you emerge from the wood, the path heads downhill towards Cross. It gets steeper here, and can be overgrown during the summer.

As you near Cross you pass through one final gate then descend a short, rocky path to the road. The White Hart is about a hundred yards away to your right.

The White Hart

Unless the lettering on the wall has been fixed, this pub is now called 'The White Hat'!

It has a very basic public bar (with a pool table) which is none too large, but an altogether more spacious lounge bar. The decor is the usual country pub mix of ancient structure/modern ornaments, but still much better than your typical town pub.

On the beer front, Ushers Best, Courage Best, Yorkshire and Founders were on offer. All but the Founders are, in my opinion, distinctly weedy beers – the Founders, though, is a different kettle of hops. It's quite heavy and rich, and extremely palatable.

The bar food menu is pretty good. Apart from the ubiquitous jacket potatoes/chips/pies there are things like steak, lemon sole and chicken stuffed with Brie to choose from. There's also a decent selection of starters and sweets if you want to make a proper meal of it.

There's a decent-sized car park across the road, plus limited roadside parking. Kids could be a problem, though, because they're not allowed in the main bars. There is a small kids' room off to one side, but the pub isn't really geared up to youngsters.

The White Hart, Cross. Lots of character and a good bar menu.

Dolebury Camp

Route: Churchill – Mendip Lodge Wood – Dolebury Camp

Distance: 4 miles

Start: The Crown, Churchill (ST 446596)

By car: Take the A371 out of Weston-super-Mare. At Banwell, turn left on to the A368, passing through Sandford to reach Churchill. Just before the traffic lights at the junction with the A38, look out for a pub called the Nelson Arms on your right. There's a turn-off here which looks as if it just leads to that pub's car park. Instead, though, it leads uphill to the Crown, which is an old stone cottage about 100 yards up the hill. There's no car park as such, but generous roadside parking.

The Walk

Dolebury Camp is not a celebrated tourist attraction, and it's not particularly visible from the surrounding countryside. It is, however, one of the Mendips' unexpected delights. It gives you excellent views of Rowberrow Warren and the surrounding countryside and is probably the most spectacular example of an Iron Age hill fort in the region.

The going is pretty easy all the way, although the tracks through the woods may be muddy after rain. There are no particularly stiff climbs, even though you do gain a fair bit of height by the time you reach Dolebury Camp.

The road leading up to The Crown curves away to the left when you approach the pub by road (the parking area is on the track straight ahead). Once you're on foot, follow this road (Skinner Lane) round and down for a hundred yards until it reaches the A38. Cross this main road, looking out for a neatly-maintained public footpath leading between two houses on the opposite side. This path leads on to a field. Head across this field diagonally to the left, where the path continues into Mendip

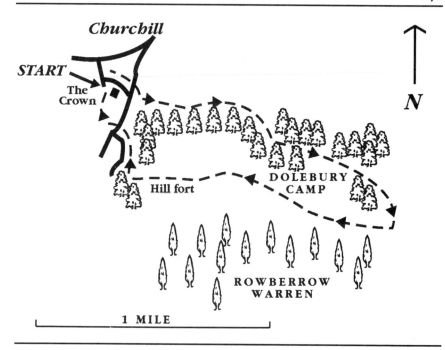

Lodge Wood. Follow this path east along the edge of the wood. About 200 yards later you come to a slightly tricky section where a track leads up to some buildings to your right. Follow the track for a few yards, looking out for a stile facing you. Climb over this and you'll see the path continuing off to the right.

The path follows the edge of the wood for a little longer, then cuts more steeply uphill. Half a mile later it joins a broad track running up the hill. Follow this track uphill (south). It gradually levels off and then starts to descend gently. To your right you'll now be able to make out the open ground of the hilltop, and just before the track enters more woodland there's a track leading off to the right which takes you out towards the Camp.

Four hundred yards later, the path divides. One route (straight ahead) skirts the ancient hill fort ahead, while the other (leading off to the right) takes you through a small copse and into the centre of the fort. This upper route means a bit more of a climb, but the views are well worth it.

Once Iron Age man populated Dolebury Camp, now it's left to grazing sheep.

The dense coniferous sweep of Rowberrow Warren to your left is especially spectacular.

By the time you reach the fort, the path is already descending. The route becomes a little unclear here, but keep heading downhill towards the trees (due west) and you should be able to pick up the path again without too much trouble. The path now curves to the right as it heads downhill, soon joining a narrow road which, in turn, leads back to the A38.

Cross the road, looking out for a public footpath sign opposite. This path takes you up a steep, stony track which then meets a broader track running across its path. Follow this track downhill to the right, and you're back at The Crown within a couple of hundred yards.

The Crown

The Crown has Character with a capital 'C'. Even the approach is odd – you first have to drive through another pub's car park (the Nelson

Arms) to get to it! It's not that it's off the beaten track, as much as the fact you could drive past it on the main road a hundred times and not realise it was there.

Inside, you'll find the pub separated into a public bar on the left, and lounge bar on the right. Both the lounge and public bars are themselves split into two areas (and levels!). In the colder weather, each one features a roaring log fire. Given that the interior is tiny anyway, it gets cosy very quickly!

The bar's stone floors and bare wooden furniture make it a very functional place indeed. The lounge is a bit more comfortable, but just as – shall we say – 'rustic'. It's cramped, not entirely comfortable and often packed out. You must find a corner, make yourself at home and expect not to be able to move a great deal. Never mind, because this is one of the most fascinating and charming pubs on the Mendips.

The Crown, Churchill. Stone floors, beer served from the wood –
a traditionalist's paradise.

You're spoilt for choice on the beer front. Butcombe is served on draught at the bar, but there is always a dazzling array of 'speciality' beers on offer, all served 'straight from the wood' behind the bar.

The Crown isn't the sort of place to go for a meal out – not unless you can eat with your elbows tucked into your ribcage – but the menu is pretty decent all the same.

Parking isn't usually a problem – there's a gravel parking area opposite the pub, plus roadside parking up the hill alongside. There is seating both in front of and behind the pub, so in the warmer weather kids can entertain themselves quite happily.

Around Shipham

Route: Shipham – Lippiatt Lane – Longbottom Farm – Winterhead Hill

Distance: 5 miles

Start: The Miners Arms, Shipham (ST 444575)

By car: From Weston-super-Mare take the A371 cast to Banwell. Here, turn off east on the A368. After three miles you reach the crossroads and traffic lights at Churchill. Turn right here, heading south along the A38. This road heads uphill and curves left then right. Just after the right-hand bend, on the left, is a garage, and just beyond that is a turn off to the left. This leads you to Shipham in around half a mile. The Miners Arms is on your right just as you come to the village centre. There's a moderately large car park behind the pub and plenty of roadside parking in the village itself.

Once a major mining region, the hills around Shipham are now used by riding stables.

The Walk

The name of the village almost certainly comes from the Anglo-Saxon words 'Ship' ('sheep') and 'Ham' ('enclosure' or 'farm'). True, agriculture was the main local industry up until the 13th century, but then mining took over. Lead, calamine, manganese, zinc, iron, copper and ochre were all mined here. Even some silver was recovered from the mineral-rich hills.

Mining is usually thought of as being a grand, industrial enterprise, but in Shipham it was very much a cottage industry. 'Mines' were dug by individuals and families rather than giant conglomerates, and could be found in the fields, streets and even people's back yards!

The mining industry peaked in the 18th century, with as many as 100 mines being worked in and around the village. This quaint way of working stretched to the method used for finding veins of ore –

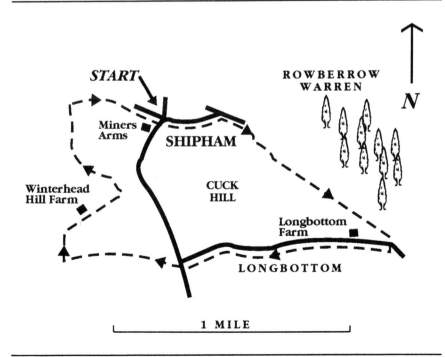

divining! The technique was introduced by German miners and was presumably successful enough to be taken up here...

From the Miners Arms, head up the lane (Hollow Road) directly opposite (to the right of the World War One memorial and across the small green). After about 300 yards the lane curves round to the left, with a smaller road carrying on straight ahead. Take this road (Barn Pool) and follow it round for about 100 yards to a T-junction. Turn right here. After about 150 yards the road narrows. To the right you'll see a large house set back from the road and, next to it, a broad track running off between hedgerows. You shortly arrive at a junction, with tracks going off to the right and left. Go left here, through the two gates ahead of you and into the field beyond.

Now then, walk a few yards out into the open and then stop to take a look around. Uphill and to the right ahead of you you'll be able to make out a stile in a wooden fence. There's an arrow on this stile pointing you across the field beyond. Head across to the fence opposite. As you draw nearer, you should be able to make out the next stile, in the right-hand corner of the fenced-off enclosure you're approaching.

By the way, if you hear a siren, followed by some loud explosions, don't imagine it's the start of World War Three. It just means that they're blasting at Shipham Quarry on the other side of the hill!

Hop over this next stile (well, *climb*, then) and cut across this enclosure to the far right-hand corner. Go over this stile and walk uphill, keeping the fence to your right. You soon come to an older, stone stile in the next corner, and an arrow pointing you diagonally across to the right. Look out for the stile in the stone wall ahead of you.

There's an arrow on this stile too, and it points you diagonally across to the left. You have to have a good sense of direction here because the hill slopes away from you and there's not much to aim for.

Ahead of you are the densely-wooded flanks of Rowberrrow Warren. It looks like something out of the Black Forest rather than a Mendip hillside.

If you've got the direction right, you should soon come to the corner of a field. On your left is a stone wall, Rowberrow Warren beyond, while ahead of you is a fence separating you from Longbottom Farm. Go through the gate in the corner to join the track on the other side.

You go right now, along a pretty mucky bridleway, through a gate and then downhill between wooden fences to a road. Be careful around this gate because the mud is about a foot deep! (I measured it. The hard way.)

You turn right here for a walk of about a mile along Long Bottom. The road isn't used much, though, so traffic's not a real problem.

When you reach the main road, head straight across on to Winscombe Drove. This is a broad, stony track which leads west first uphill and then, after a level section, gently downhill again. About half a mile from the main road a track leads off to the right, towards Winterhead Hill Farm. The farm buildings shortly come into view and there's a left-hand bend in the track. On the right, on this bend, is a gate. Go through (or over) this gate and head across the field beyond, aiming just to the left of the top right-hand corner. Here you'll find a stone stile. Go over the stile, then follow the left-hand edge of the next field. You now get great views across the countryside towards Sandford Hill to the left, while ahead of you is Shipham, lying on the western slopes of Cuck Hill.

The path now starts descending more steeply towards a wooded section in the bottom of the valley ahead of you. Just as the path looks like becoming too steep to follow, it comes to a broader track running across your path. Go left here, through the gate, to follow the edge of the valley, with a fence and a wood on your right.

Go through the next gate, and cut across the open ground beyond, still following the track. Shortly, it forks away slightly to the right and downhill, towards a gap in the trees ahead. Here you'll find a gate and, beyond that, a hedge-lined track alongside a small brook.

Before long, this track brings you out amidst some houses. Carry on, ignoring the first track you see leading off to the right but taking the second, next to a large, white house. This track leads you east up over the hill and back towards Shipham. As the track levels off you reach a T-junction. Take the track off to the right. You shortly arrive at the outskirts of Shipham. Turn left through an iron gate and you find yourself in a housing estate. Head straight up the road facing you and, within a few hundred yards, you'll find yourself back at the main road leading through Shipham. The Miners Arms is just a few yards away on the right.

The Miners Arms

The Miners Arms is an unpretentious little village pub which concentrates more on basic amenities – tables, beer and food – than fancy decor and piped music.

You can tell from the moment you walk in the door that it's a 'locals' pub, although you won't get the freezing stares you get in most – it's a lot friendlier than that.

The bar is ahead of you as you walk in. To the right is a snug little seating area, to the left a larger bar area and, beyond that, tables laid out for eating.

The Miner's Arms, Shipham. Few frills, but a good basic bar menu and a choice of beers.

The menu is standard pub-grub stuff, but the prices are pretty reasonable. Food is served both at lunchtimes and during the evening, and on Friday nights you can eat accompanied by live music (a pleasure I was regrettably forced to forgo).

There are a couple of interesting beers to choose from, too. Smiles bitter almost lives up to its name – it's pleasantly, er, pleasant – but 'Tanglefoot' is altogether more drinkable.

Basically, it's a pretty good pub for walkers – you won't feel as if you have to check your appearance in a mirror before you go in. Being a locals pub, it can get a bit 'cliquey', but if you don't mind that, you can take the opportunity to down a couple of interesting pints, take on board a plateful of grub and generally relax after a sturdy walk around the Shipham hills.

Around Axbridge

Route: Axbridge – Cheddar Reservoir – Cheddar Wood

Distance: 2 miles

Start: The Almshouse Tavern, Axbridge (ST 432545)

By car: From Weston-super-Mare, take the A370 south to East Brent, then take the first exit at the roundabout to head north-east on the A38. At Cross, turn right, following the signs to Axbridge. The town itself is about a mile along this road. There is some parking space in the main square, but it's often full. There are other small (signposted) car parks nearby.

The Walk

Axbridge is a fascinating little medieval town which still retains much of its character despite those two 20th century malaises: tourism and the motor car. The main square is a very pretty spot, but it's also the town's main night-spot, so don't expect too much peace and quiet. Just off the main square, up a flight of broad stone steps, is the church of St. John. A short walk away is Cheddar Reservoir which is open to the public and, in good weather, plays host to a myriad of brightly-coloured sailboards and dinghies.

Meanwhile, on the other side of the A371, a short climb will take you up on to the slopes of Fry's Hill, from where you get an excellent view of the man-made reservoir and the countryside beyond.

Axbridge is a bit of a historical curiosity these days, but a thousand years ago it was an important town – it even had a mint. The source of the name is not really known. It certainly derives in part from the nearby river Axe, but the town is a long way from any possible bridge over the river. It's more likely that it got its name through overlooking the Axe at a strategically useful, elevated site. (There was a royal palace to protect at Cheddar.)

Since then, the village has been in decline. Its strategic value is gone, since we are no longer – we hope – at risk from an invasion of Danes (except by air-conditioned coach). Commercially, too, Axbridge has faded into relative insignificance. The Victorians planted the first of the Mendip strawberries here in the 1870s, and there was once a railway line. The line is gone, but the station buildings still stand.

While the village gets its name from medieval times, the Romans were here before then (as they were in most places on the Mendips). Evidence comes from the discovery of a Roman skeleton here as recently as 1982.

The Almshouse Tavern is a few yards down Moorland Street, which leads off south from the main square. If you carry on down this road, you'll find, after 200-300 yards, it curves round to the left. Keep on walking and look out for a gate at the end of the road, in another 200-300 yards. Once through the gate, follow the track on the other side

The hills above Axbridge give sweeping views over the man-made Cheddar Reservoir.

through another gate and then across some rough pasture to a third gate to the left of a low building.

The track now leads past a row of trees, joining the road that leads up to the reservoir entrance. There's a stile here for pedestrians, and it's well worth taking a few moments to walk up the reservoir embankment and take in the view.

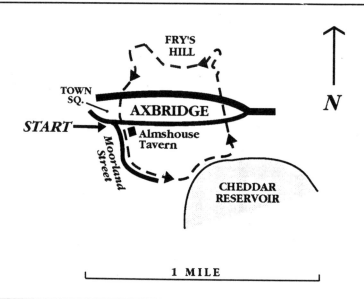

The reservoir is a man-made lake built in 1938. It holds 1,300 million gallons of water and is fed by the Mendip hills. You can walk all around the edge, but there are only two access points – the site is owned and controlled by Bristol Water.

Ready to move on? Take the lane that leads north between two well-kept rows of trees. When you get to the road, cross straight over. Within a few yards you'll arrive at another, busier, road – the A371. Cross this too, and head up the track opposite. This track gradually narrows, but remains very clear. After a quarter of a mile you come to a gate, and beyond this gate take the path which heads to the left (west). This leads you along the southern slopes of Fry's Hill, and gives you excellent views over the reservoir.

Half a mile later you join a track which leads back downhill towards Axbridge. You come out at the A371 again more or less opposite Axbridge church. Cut through the churchyard and you'll emerge back in Axbridge's main square.

The Almshouse Tavern

The Almshouse Tavern is a rather inconspicuous little pub just off Axbridge's main square. You realise it's not so little, though, when you open the heavy wooden door and step inside.

Ahead of you is the bar, while to the right is a modest seating area. To the left is the pub's restaurant, which is quite large, and there is more restaurant seating upstairs in the gallery. Accommodation is also available.

Basically, the Almshouse Tavern is more of a hotel/restaurant with a bar than a pub. You certainly couldn't get many people at a time in the bar. That's the bad news. The good news is that it's a really quaint old place with bags of character. But it's not one of these dimly lit Gothic mausoleums that most people associate with 'character'. Instead, it's well lit and quite comfortable – if a bit posh.

Which means that any muddy walking books and sodden anoraks should be left in the car. Neither is there any beer on draught, alas. But what is good is the menu. It's way above usual pub grub standards and includes lots of unusual starters and snacks and a wide choice of main meals. You can go for any of a range of steaks or tackle something more exotic, like trout in almonds, for example.

A pretty fancy menu, then, so does that mean fancy prices? Not at all. Considering what's on the menu, the prices are very reasonable indeed – little more than the standard 'chips-with-everything' pub prices.

The Almshouse Tavern is not the place to go for a boozy night out, or somewhere to take a party of mud-splattered hikers. But after a gentle walk around Axbridge and its environs it provides a cosy, genial atmosphere with some excellent food and lots of character.

There's only one slight problem – parking. Axbridge is second only to Cheddar and Wells for parking problems. There are spaces in the main square, but you'd be lucky to find any free. The only real alternative is a nearby pay-and-display car park. Neither is there any garden – a bit too much to ask for in a crowded town centre, really.

The Almshouse Tavern, Axbridge. More of a restaurant than a bar –
a great place to eat.

Introduction to the Mendip Lakes

The Walks

Chew Valley Lake From The Pelican Inn, Chew Magna (ST 576632)

Litton Reservoir   From The King's Arms, Litton (ST 593546)

Blagdon   From The New Inn, Blagdon (ST 505590)

Compton Martin   From The Ring O' Bells, Compton Martin (ST 543571)

The Area

The Mendip Hills aren't all steep hills and looming forests. To the north are a series of man-made reservoirs, the two most obvious being Blagdon Reservoir and Chew Valley Lake.

Blagdon Reservoir is, unfortunately, closed to the public, but the meadows and farmland between it and the slopes of the Mendips offer very pleasant walking, as well as occasional views across the water.

Chew Valley Lake is a different proposition. It's much larger, for a start, and public access is allowed at several points – including one purpose-built picnic site. The lake is a haven for wildlife and attracts as many birdwatchers as holiday-makers.

These are the two best-known reservoirs, but there is a third reservoir to the east, tucked away behind the little village of Litton. It's so tucked away, in fact, that no-one without an Ordnance Survey map and a keen eye would ever suspect that Litton reservoir existed. And yet it's one of the prettiest and most secluded spots on the Mendips, and there is a public footpath along its entire length.

The lakes aren't the only attraction of this part of the Mendips, though – there's also the village of Compton Martin which, for my money, is one of the most attractive in the region. Not least because of its idyllic little village duckpond. It also has one of the best Mendip pubs – the Ring O' Bells. And just a short walk up through Compton Wood leads out on to the northern edge of the Mendip plateau, from where you get excellent views north over the lakes.

Chew Valley Lake

Route: Chew Magna – Knowle Hill – Chew Valley Lake – River Chew

Distance: 6 miles

Start: The Pelican Inn, Chew Magna (ST 576632)

By car: From the Weston-super-Mare direction, follow the A368 Bath road westwards (or eastwards, if you're coming from the other direction) to West Harptree. From there head north along the B3114 past the lake, through Chew Stoke and into Chew Magna. The Pelican is on your right in the centre of the village, and there is a moderately large free car park here too.

The Walk

Chew Magna is a few miles north of the northern edge of the Mendips, but I still class it as part of the region. Not least because it's a great starting point from which to explore Chew Valley Lake, which nestles right at the base of the Mendips and is a great place to stroll, lay out a picnic and study the abundant waterfowl which make the lake their home.

Chew Magna is also the starting point for one of my favourite walks in the region. There are few hills, few dramatic outlooks, just lots of very pleasant, very varied walking in some of the prettiest countryside anywhere.

From the Pelican, turn right to the crossroads in the centre of the village, then take the road heading right (south) down towards the lake. Within a quarter of a mile, this road curves round to the left, but a narrower lane heads on straight ahead – Denny Lane.

Follow Denny Lane uphill for a couple of hundred yards, then, with the houses behind you and nearing the top, look for a gap in the hedge to your left and a public footpath. This track leads you between hedgerows (it can get a little overgrown in the summer) to a stile. Beyond this stile the track is much wider.

Chew Valley Lake is a mecca for birdwatchers in the region, as well as a favourite picnic site.

Follow this grassy track (with Knowle Hill visible up ahead) down towards Knowle Hill Farm, through a gate, and then keeping to the left of the field beyond, passing to the right of the farm buildings. You climb the slope beyond, still keeping to the edge of the field, to a stile in the corner. There's a public footpath sign here to show you're on the right route.

You climb a narrow track uphill now, with a tall garden fence on your left, then emerge on to a broad grassy track and turn left, joining the track leading away from Far End Cottage (the house you've just circled). This track leads around the northern edge of Knowle Hill, while we want to cut across it. So, once the track has curved round first to the right, then to the left, look out for a track leading off to the right across the hill and towards the lake (south).

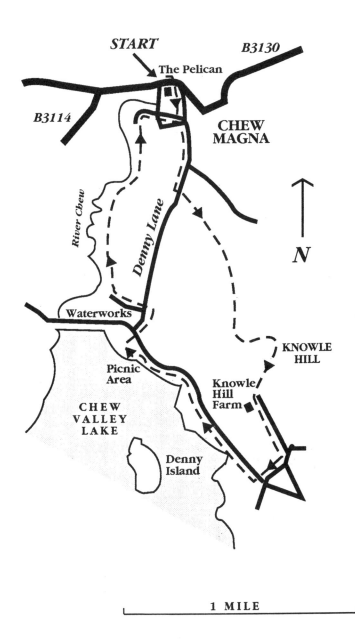

Knowle Hill turns out to be a miniature windswept moorland of bracken and rough grass – rather a nice surprise in the midst of such cultivated, even tame, countryside. It's criss-crossed by so many paths that it's practically impossible to describe a specific route, though. So the best thing to do is aim across the hill broadly in the direction of the lake.

A path runs along the southern edge of Knowle Hill, and any path you take across the hill will bring you out on to it at one point or another. From here, head south to join the road running past Knowle Hill Farm.

Stay on this road, heading downhill until, in about a quarter of a mile, the road curves round to the right. Then, a little further on, you'll see a turn-off to the right. Go right here.

You're now on the road which joins Bishop Sutton and Chew Magna, and which runs alongside the lake. There are a couple of picnic areas on this road and a whole network of walkways. Now here's something rather silly. The first proper entrance to the lakeside is a good 400-600 yards up the road. And yet there are public footpaths by the lake edge just the other side of the fence to your left as you walk. There's even a gate in the fence, but it's kept locked! Far be it from me to encourage such things, but it occurs to me that walkers used to negotiating stiles have few problems negotiating locked gates. Just an observation, you understand.

You can follow the lakeside all the way to the dam at the northern end of the lake. There are a couple of temptations en route, though, including an ice cream van and, further on, a cafe. Here, you leave the lakeside via the path out to the road, and then cross over to Denny Lane. Just to the left of the lane there's a footpath signpost here which indicates the 'Two Rivers' route and a stile. Hop over the stile and follow the field edge parallel with Denny Lane until you reach a broad, metalled track. Follow the signpost, heading left along the track. At the bottom of the slope, the track carries on but a signpost directs you off to the right.

You now head right through a small wood, over a tiny bridge and another stile, and then out into the open again. You're now following the course of the River Chew – at least as far as it is possible to, since the Chew weaves through the countryside like an inebriated grass snake.

From here you head back towards Chew Magna via the signposted route. There are numerous stiles and changes of direction, so observe the way the arrows on the stiles point very carefully. Always remember that you are, basically, following the right hand bank of the river, and you won't go too far wrong.

Eventually you round the last twist in the river and arrive at a gateway onto a track leading into the village. Go right here, as the arrow indicates, and you join a lane which leads you out onto the road between Chew Magna and the lake. Go right here, retracing your steps, and turn left at the crossroads in the village to find yourself back outside the Pelican Inn.

The Pelican Inn

The Pelican Inn looks ever so slightly grotty from the outside, but appearances can be deceptive. Inside, there are two bars. To the right is the Lounge Bar, to the left the Public Bar.

The Pelican Inn, Chew Magna. A very attractive lounge, cosy during those darker evenings

The Lounge Bar is a long room featuring cosy furnishings and an even cosier real log fire! And here's a novelty – the bar has a thatched roof! The overall effect on a darkening autumn evening after a brisk walk is extremely mellowing and enjoyable.

The beer choice consists of what seems to be rapidly becoming the standard Mendip line-up – Ushers Best, Courage Best and Founders Ale. Ushers Best and Courage Best should only be contemplated if you have a powerful thirst and no palate. The best of the trio by far is the Founders. It's just a pity that more Mendip pubs don't experiment with 'guest beers'.

On the food front, you could be disappointed. Not with the choice or quality but with the availability – the menu (standard pub stuff like chicken & chips, ploughman's, sandwiches etc) is only served at lunchtimes. Ah well.

The Public Bar is a rather more basic version of the Lounge. If you arrive looking like you've just been through a hedge backwards, this may be the better bet.

Chew Magna is an unexpectedly attractive little village tucked away in the back of beyond, and the Lounge Bar of the Pelican is an unexpectedly cosy little haven when you get there.

Litton Reservoir

Route: Litton – Upper Reservoir – Lower Reservoir – Sherborne

Distance: 2 miles

Start: The King's Arms, Litton (ST 593546)

By car: From Weston-super-Mare, take the A371 east to Banwell, turning off on to the A368. Follow this to Churchill, head straight across at the traffic lights and carry on eastwards. The road winds its way through Rickford, Blagdon, Ubley and Compton Martin and then West Harptree. As the road curves sharply to the left on leaving West Harptree, take the turning on the right. The village of Litton is about three miles along this road, and the King's Arms is on the main road, on the left-hand side. It has a large car park and gardens, and is difficult to miss.

The Walk

This area is renowned for its two major reservoirs – Blagdon Reservoir and Chew Valley Lake. Few people, however, are aware of the existence of the much smaller, but very picturesque, Litton Reservoir. This is hidden away amongst the hills just to the north of Litton village.

The reservoir is actually split into two parts – the Upper and Lower reservoirs – by a dam. You can walk alongside both reservoirs, crossing the dam in the process.

You can usually expect to have the place to yourself (except in the best of weather and at weekends) because it's so secluded and little-known, and you get to see a lot of scenery in a short walk.

From the King's Arms, head right along the main road, then go right at the next junction to follow the road downhill into Litton village. At the bottom of the hill, the road goes right and then, a few yards further on, it turns right again to head back in the direction of the main road. At this second corner you'll see a track leading off to the left. This is the way you want to go.

Litton Reservoir offers a little known and very tranquil lakeside walk.

There's a Public Footpath signpost here, directing you to a wooden stile just ahead. Climb over this stile and head across the field beyond. To your left you'll see a little river. This is in fact the river Chew, which you'll also meet if you do the Chew Magna walk.

On the other side of this field you'll come to a fence. Don't head for the gate in the left-hand corner. Instead, look for a stile ahead of you and slightly to the right. Climb over the stile (mind the mud!) and follow the left-hand edge of the field beyond. You shortly come to another stile. On the other side of this one you'll see a last stile just across the grass. This takes you out on to a lane.

Now, you have to be a bit careful here. The track picks up again directly opposite on the other side of the lane. But you don't go through the gate facing you and slightly to the right, which seems the most obvious route. Instead, look for a narrow gap in the hedge directly facing you. If you slip through this you find yourself on a narrow track which heads off to the left and the right. Go right.

This track gradually curves round to the left. Before long you find yourself on the banks of the upper reservoir. If you have children or dogs with you, make sure you keep an eye on them, because in places the path goes very close to the bank at the edge of the water, and it would be very easy to fall in!

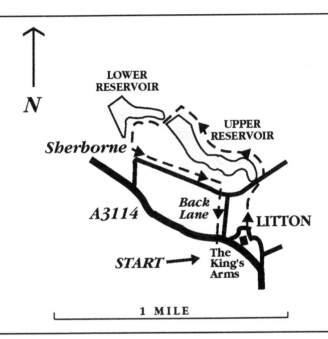

After about a quarter of a mile you come to the dam separating the Upper and Lower reservoirs. The view from here is quite spectacular in its own little way – there's quite a height difference between the two reservoirs. You get a good view across the Lower Litton Reservoir towards East Harptree and the northern slopes of the Mendips.

You walk across the dam now, crossing a large concrete slip-way on the other side via a metal bridge and then turning right to follow the footpath downhill towards the Lower Reservoir.

The path alongside the Lower Reservoir is less distinct, but still easy to follow. Within a few hundred yards it's winding its way towards

Sherborne. The path can get a bit marshy and overgrown as you near the village. After negotiating a couple of stiles you arrive at a grassy clearing. Go left here, joining a metalled lane. You soon come to a T-junction, where the lane joins another road on the corner of a hair-pin bend. Go straight ahead here.

You're now heading along Whitehouse Lane, back towards Litton. About a quarter of a mile later, Whitehouse Lane starts heading downhill. Just as you're nearing a left-hand bend you'll see a turning off to the right. This is Back Lane, and it leads you out on to the main road, right next to the King's Arms.

The Kings Arms, Litton. Built in the fifteenth century, the insides are a maze!

The King's Arms

The King's Arms is one of the finest country pubs on the Mendips. Admittedly, its rustic charm owes more to tourism than any innate rural appeal, but there's no denying the place is beautifully decorated and run very well indeed.

It's set a little way back from the road in a little dip, and you enter it after first walking through its exquisitely maintained gardens and then descending a short flight of stone steps. Inside you find yourself in a labyrinth of tiny rooms which meander eventually, if you head left, to the bar. (To the right is the restaurant.)

This pub sells lots of very good food. The existence of the restaurant is one clue. Being faced with a wall-sized specials board the moment you walk in the door is another! The food here is not especially cheap, but the menu is extra-special. It even includes escargots, a delicacy I have never, and *will* never sample!

It's a bit difficult to describe the layout of the rooms. There is only one bar, but around it are at least six little room-lets, each on a different level, each with its own character.

Or, if you don't fancy being cooped up indoors on a fine summer's evening there's always the garden. It's the sort of place that looks idyllic as you drive past in the car, but can get tiresome when you're sharing it with three dozen people! It's the same with all pub gardens, though.

Kids are welcome both in the garden and in the designated areas inside the pub.

The King's Arms does, however, have one single, huge failing. NO REAL ALE. Appalling, and a real fly in the ointment for those whose digestive systems are unable to cope with the pressurised, pasteurised and altogether pulverised offerings from the keg beer manufacturers.

Nevertheless, the King's Arms is one of the most attractive pubs in the Mendips and offers one of the finest menus. Real ale drinkers will just have to grin and bear it.

Blagdon

Route: Blagdon – Holt Farm – Ubley Hatchery – Ubley – Blagdon

Distance: 5 miles

Start: The New Inn, Blagdon (ST 505590)

By car: Take the A371 out of Weston-super-Mare to Banwell, then turn off east on the A368. Three miles along this road you reach a crossroads at Churchill. Head straight across. Blagdon is about three miles further on. The road twists and turns a great deal as it goes through the village. Look out for a sign indicating free parking to the left as the road turns sharp right uphill. Alternatively, follow the road uphill then left and take the next turning on the left. The New Inn is a little way down this road on the right, and has a large car park.

The Walk

Blagdon lies below the northern slopes of the Mendips, overlooking Blagdon Lake reservoir. The reservoir is owned by Bristol Water, and there's no public access to the lake edges. However, there is some pleasant walking between the lake edges and the slopes of the Mendip hills, plus a visit to Ubley, a very attractive village lying largely away from the main road. Ubley has a decent pub, too, just in case you can't make it all the way back to Blagdon without refreshment...

From the New Inn, walk uphill, away from the lake. As the road curves round to the left, look out for a turning on the left. It's called Grib Lane. Follow Grib Lane to its end, where you'll see a Public Footpath sign. Carry on down this grassy track, looking out for a small gate to your left.

You climb over this gate to descend beneath some trees towards the lake. You shortly emerge at a stile and an arrow directing you straight

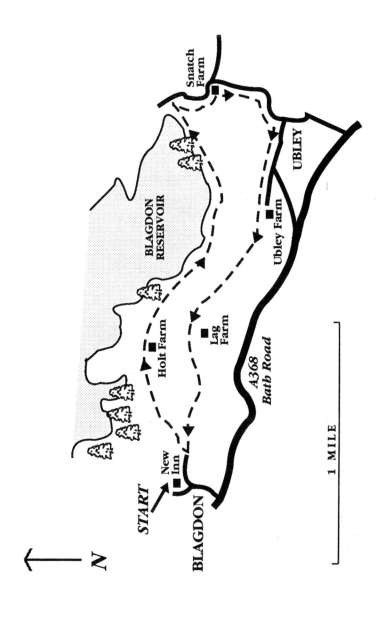

ahead. Once over the stile, follow the right hand edge of the field all the way down to the gate at the bottom.

Go through the gate, then head right along the farm track. This can get decidedly muddy after rain! As you near Holt Farm you come to another gate. Just beyond this gate, to the left, is a stile and an arrow pointing you on your way. Climb over the stile, then head diagonally across the field beyond, aiming for two trees next to the corner of the farm buildings. Here you'll find another stile. Follow the right hand edge of the field around the back of the farm buildings, then keep going to the corner of the field, where you'll find another stile... and some more mud, if you've been unlucky with the weather. (Holt Farm boasts a large herd of cows, creatures which have an unparalleled ability to turn lush grasslands into quagmires.) Once over this stile, you'll see another immediately to your left. Climb this one and then carry on along the left-hand edge of the field beyond.

With Holt Farm now out of the way, the going is much more pleasant. When you reach the corner of the field you'll see another stile. This takes

The meadows around Blagdon provide some excellent rural walking.

you on to a footpath running next to a private road, and this footpath then leads to another stile... keep heading in the same direction and you'll have no problem finding the stiles. There are another half-dozen between you and the road by Ubley Hatchery.

Once you reach the road, turn right. The road takes you south and then east to Snatch Farm, where there's a turning to the right and a footpath sign. You can either take the road or the footpath (they run parallel with each other and then join up again at Park Farm). The footpath is a bit more pleasant, but has no obvious exit at the other end...

From Park Farm, follow the road into Ubley, then turn right in the village centre. As the road leaves the village, it turns sharp right. You carry straight on, past a No Through Road sign towards Ubley Farm. You'll soon see a Public Footpath sign to confirm you're on the right route. Passing the farmhouse on your left, go through the gate at the end of the track and then follow the gravel track beyond round to an unmarked wooden gate. Once through the gate, head left along the field edge to another gate in the hedge facing you.

From here, it gets slightly trickier. Strike out diagonally across this field to a stile in the far right-hand corner. Once over this, look out for another stile across the field, slightly to the right. So far so good. From here, follow the left-hand edge of the field, then, when it opens out, strike out for a large metal gate in the hedge on the other side. Go through this gate, crunch your way across a small gravelled parking area and look out for the stile and footpath sign facing you on the other side.

Cross the track on the other side, hop over another stile and you're now on a grassy path which leads to . . . yes, another stile. The arrow on this one points you across the field beyond. On the other side, you pick up a gravel track, following it round to the left as it curves first left then right along the field edge. At this point you should be looking out for a fairly prominent stile and footpath marker next to a metal gate on your right. Climb over, then go left, following the left edge of the field. You know there's not far to go now, as you see the spire of Blagdon church rising above the hillside ahead of you. In the left-hand corner of this field you'll find another stile. Carry on round the edge of the field, and then take the stile that appears on your left.

If you are doing this walk in the summer, you are now entering the nettle capital of Europe; fortunately, this decidedly overgrown uphill section doesn't last long, because you soon rejoin Grib Lane. It's now only a short walk back to the pub.

The New Inn, Blagdon. A busy pub with a good menu and great views across the lakes from the garden.

The New Inn

The New Inn is what I would call a busy 'food pub'. The sort of place you go to for an early evening out, or for a pub lunch at the weekend. It's got a decent enough menu, a very good-sized car park and a superb setting, overlooking Blagdon Lake.

Walking inside from the car park/garden, you find yourself in a long, narrow bar. To the right is seating for a dozen or so, to the left are some smaller tables along the wall facing the bar. Beyond the bar, on the far left, is a smaller room big enough for about a dozen people.

This place can get pretty busy at peak times. The menu even warns you about it, suggesting that delays can occur and if you can't wait that you simply call again another day. Hmm... you can get away with that sort of thing if the menu is something special.

Well, the menu is good for a pub, but not special. There are, in particular, lots of starters and snacks to choose from – including toasted sandwiches. Look out too for a specials board alongside the bar.

Probably what makes the New Inn so popular is the view from the garden. Blagdon Lake really is a very pretty sight, set as it is in the middle of picturesque green farmland.

One hopes the kids are equally transfixed by the scenery, because no-one under 14 is allowed in the bars. Fortunately, there's enough in the garden to occupy them for an hour or so.

The beer choice is pretty good. Wadworths 6X is a decent pint, if a little acid at times, or you can drink a pint of Bass (I would if I were you). Wadworths IPA is also on draught (I don't know this one).

The New Inn is a large, busy and attractive country pub. At mealtimes, though, it's somewhere to quickly feed your face and leave. Somehow, it's not the sort of place you linger at – probably something to do with the non-stop throughput of customers.

Compton Martin

Route: Compton Martin – Compton Combe – The Wrangle – Highfield Lane

Distance: 2 miles

Start: The Ring O' Bells, Compton Martin (ST 543571)

By car: From Weston-Super-Mare, take the A371 east to Banwell, then turn off on to the A368. Go straight across the traffic lights at Churchill and carry on along the A368 through Rickford, Blagdon and Ubley. Compton Martin is about a mile beyond Ubley, and the Ring O' Bells is on the right just inside the village.

The view from the hill above Compton Martin encompasses Chew Valley Lake to the north.

The Walk

Compton Martin is one of the most picturesque villages on the Mendips, not least because of its really quaint village duckpond. To the north are the reservoirs of Blagdon Lake and Chew Valley Lake, but our walk heads south, up the thickly wooded northern slopes of the Mendips out on to the Mendip plateau, from where you get a breathtaking view across Chew Valley Lake. You then head downhill and back to the village via twisting, picturesque country lanes.

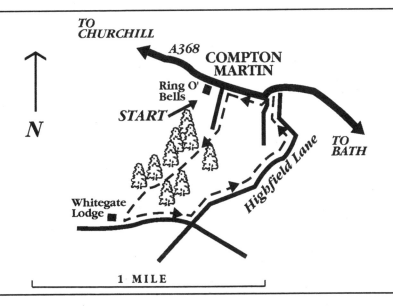

From the Ring O' Bells, turn right, then immediately right again up a narrow road leading uphill towards the woods and a cluster of cottages.

On the other side of these houses, the road turns into a track heading uphill towards Compton Combe. It's pretty steep, but even after rain the going is still generally good. Before long the track emerges into Cliff Quarry, which is now disused. Keep to the left of the clearing, picking up the track again in the upper left-hand corner.

From here the track leads more or less directly uphill through the combe. You're walking through an old deciduous wood, and there are quite a few trees down across the track. None completely block your path, though. Keeping on walking, negotiating a couple of stiles on the way, and eventually the track levels out and grows narrower. Before long you emerge into the open, facing a wooden stile. Ahead of you, on the other side of the stile, is Whitegate Lodge which looks from here like private property, but the footpath does indeed cross the grass and join its driveway. It's just a few short paces to the road from here.

Turn left now, and head west along the road. Just a few hundred yards later you come to a crossroads. Turn left here and start the descent back down to Compton Martin. It's from here that you get the best views of Chew Valley Lake way over to the north east.

This road is called Highfield Lane, and passes between some extremely well-to-do properties with superb views. You'd need a bit of cash to move in here, though. (Don't forget to recommend this book to your friends. Ahem.)

Lower down, the road steepens, the high hedgerows closing in around you. After a few more twists and turns, Highfield Lane emerges on the main Bath road. Go left here, following the road back down into Compton Martin. The Ring O' Bells is now just a couple of hundred yards away on the left hand side of the road.

The Ring O' Bells

The Ring O' Bells is arguably the best pub on the Mendips. The Crown at Churchill has more rustic character (and an astonishing choice of beers), the Sun Inn at Whatley the most attractive garden setting, and a handful of other pubs feature a more exotic menu – but none combine every element so successfully!

The Ring O' Bells *looks* like a twee little country pub from the road. It's not until you step inside you realise how large it is. To the left is a medium-sized and pretty raucous 'locals' bar, while to the right is a quieter lounge area. Beyond this, extending to the back of the pub is a large eating area.

Behind the pub is a truly huge garden, complete with swings, slides and climbing frame, while to the side is a car park big enough to cope with all but the busiest sessions.

The inside is really nicely decorated. Not too fancy, not too modern. A good mixture of the traditional and the comfortable. Beer choice is modest but adequate – Wadworths 6X (good), Butcombe (lots swear by it) and Bass (excellent).

The menu is very good indeed. All the usual pub fare can be found here, plus some more adventurous dishes like Jambalaya (a spicy, rice-based Creole dish) and the pub's own home-made chicken and chestnut paté. You can also sample some pretty calorific home-made sweets, if your waistline can stand it.

If the weather's bad you can bring kids inside. There is a 'family room' at the back of the pub but, like family rooms everywhere, there's always one extremely unpleasant little brat that runs around screaming and knocking things over.

The Ring O' Bells has got everything – character, good food, good beer, parking and a garden. It's an excellent 'summer evening' pub, and one of the best on the Mendips.

The Ring O' Bells, Compton Martin. A great menu, good beers and a terrific atmosphere.

Introduction to the Central Mendips

The Walks

Black Down   From The Swan, Rowberrow (ST 452583)

Burrington Ham   From The Plume of Feathers, Rickford (ST 487593)

Cheddar Gorge   From The Galleries Inn, Cheddar Gorge (ST463538)

Around Priddy   From The New Inn, Priddy (ST 527510)

Stockhill Plantation From Castle of Comfort Inn (ST 544532)

Westbury Beacon   From The Rodney Stoke Inn, Rodney Stoke
                      (ST 484503)

The Area

The central Mendip region contains some of the Mendips' most memorable walking. The more spectacular hills are to the west; this is a region of misty upland plateaus, thick, coniferous forest, dramatic views and, of course, the famous Cheddar Gorge.

While most of the Mendips are open farmland, there are two very substantial forestry plantations in the central region. Both are owned and run by the Forestry Commission, and both are open to the public and feature lots of well-defined tracks.

Rowberrow Warren is the largest and most spectacular. It takes up a large area just below and to the west of Black Down, the Mendips' highest point, and offers some excellent walking more reminiscent of European forests than English hills. Black Down is a stark contrast after this forest, a bare, windswept moor rising high above the surrounding landscape.

The second forest is the Stockhill Plantation, right in the middle of the Mendip plateau near the village of Priddy. It's essentially flat and there are no streams to follow (unlike Rowberrow Warren) but if anything the forest is denser.

But the place most tourists come to see is undoubtedly Cheddar Gorge. The trouble is, most only see it from the bottom, not realising that there is a cliff-top path all along the eastern cliffs. Even fewer folk realise there is another path down the western side that offers, at one point, a truly spectacular view of the gorge.

Burrington Combe is a kind of poor relation to Cheddar Gorge but is still spectacular in its own way. And just over the hill is the tiny hamlet of Rickford, which has to be one of the most charmingly rustic little settlements in the area.

Right at the centre of the Mendip plateau is the isolated little village of Priddy. It's a fairly grim spot at the best of times, but makes a great base from which to explore the old mine workings at St. Cuthberts (started by the Romans) and North Hill, site of the Priddy Nine Barrows, ancient burial mounds up to 3,000 years old, and amongst the best examples of their type in the country.

Meanwhile, a little to the west, the central plateau falls away towards the Somerset flatlands and the village of Rodney Stoke. From this village you can climb up on to the plateau via the ancient hill fort on Westbury beacon and take in the wide open landscapes and huge skies before heading back down to Rodney Stoke, enjoying the breathtaking views as you do so.

Black Down

Route: Rowberrow Warren – Tynings Farm – Black Down – Burrington Combe – Rowberrow Warren

Distance: 8 miles

Start: The Swan, Rowberrow (ST 452583)

By car: From Weston-super-Mare, take the A371, heading east to Banwell. At Banwell, turn left on to the A368, still heading east. When you arrive at the crossroads at Churchill, turn right. Within a mile the road will curve uphill and to the left. At the top of this hill the road will curve sharply right. Take the small turning on your left at this point. The Swan is about half a mile up this road, on your left. There is a medium-sized car park alongside the pub and a large car park on the opposite side of the road.

The Walk

Black Down is one of the landmarks of the Mendips. It's a great, rolling mass which looms above the surrounding hills. Its most striking feature at most times of year, however, is not its height (it's the highest point in the area at 1,060 feet) but its colour. At some times of year it *can* be almost black, thanks to the gorse and bracken that covers the summit. At other times it takes on a deep brown colour that stands out against the muted greens and browns of the surrounding hills.

Mining has been big business throughout the centuries on the Mendips, and Rowberrow didn't escape the prospectors. Calamine was found and mined here – calamine was an essential mineral for the brass and zinc industries of the eighteenth century.

As well as Black Down, the walk also takes in the dense, coniferous forest of Rowberrow Warren. The land was taken over by the Forestry Commission in the 1930s, when it was covered with bracken. Now, though, it's a dense plantation of conifers, mainly spruce and larch. Be

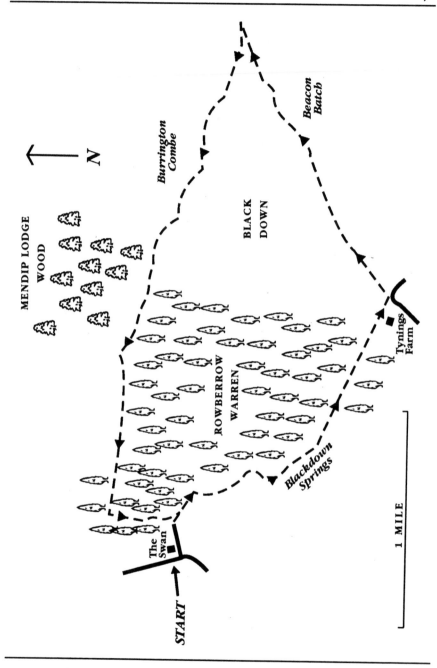

very wary of forest fires in the summer. In 1957, 150 acres of forest were destroyed by one such fire. There are many very attractive paths through the forest, which are popular with both walkers and horse riders.

This is one thing to watch out for. Horses tend to churn up the tracks quite badly after rain, so good footwear is definitely to be recommended – boots if possible. However, it's worth it. The forest walks through Rowberrow Warren are peaceful and very pleasant, with the views and unexpected wildness of Black Down a striking contrast afterwards.

From the car park facing the Swan pub, cross the road and take the side-road heading off past the side of the pub. This is School Lane. It takes you downhill between a few houses and into a little wooded valley with a stream running through it (useful for rinsing off muddy boots on the way back!). Keep going and you will shortly come to a fork in the track. One track leads ahead and uphill, the other curves away to the left. Take the left hand track. Carry on walking through the valley, towards more houses. Once past these you reach a gateway marking the boundary of the Forestry Commission plantation, about half a mile from your start point.

The path carries on through a very pleasant little valley alongside a stream; it can get very muddy here. Nevertheless, it's still one of the most picturesque parts of the forest. Look out for a small enclosure owned by Bristol Waterworks. This marks an underground reservoir with a capacity of 80,000 gallons. The water comes from underground springs – Blackdown Springs, the stream running alongside the path, is only used in emergencies. This stream might not look much most of the time, but it can flow at up to 130,000 gallons a day. However, it doesn't flow anywhere! Instead, it disappears down a number of holes, or 'swallets', in the Mendip limestone. Limestone is a soluble rock, readily attacked and dissolved by water. Indeed, the whole Mendip range is a honeycomb of underground passages.

Within a few hundred yards the path and the trees open out a little. The going underfoot can still be very muddy, though. In another few hundred yards, and about a mile from the start of your walk, you reach a small clearing and a fork in the path. A wide track leads off to the left, while a smaller one leads off ahead. This is signposted 'Black Down', and it's the one we want.

From here you'll be climbing upwards and out of the forest (in a little under a mile). For a while, though, you're still following the course of a stream, and the going stays muddy. But then you will see another signpost to Black Down, pointing you towards the left, crossing the stream. The track leads uphill, between the trees. From here you're climbing a broad, stony track and the going is much better.

Rowberrow Warren is the largest coniferous forest on the Mendips and has plenty of paths.

Rowberrow Warren is a 'working' forest, so don't be surprised to find whole areas of trees cut down. There are a number of gravel roads running through the forest marked 'Private'; these are used by the forestry vehicles.

Half a mile later you emerge abruptly from the forest. Look out for some more muddy going just before the end. As you emerge from the forest you'll see Tynings Farm (a major Mendip riding centre) ahead of you. Keep following the track you're on – to your left you'll see the broad mass of Black Down. Keep to the track, zigzagging your way between the farm buildings.

Tyning's Farm is one of the oldest farms in the region, and its name comes from the Saxon and means 'enclosed' or 'fenced fields'. Nearby is Tyning's Barrows Swallet. This cave system was undiscovered until 1968, when a storm cause ground movement which exposed the entrance. It's over three-quarters of a mile long and reaches a depth of 430 feet. It's one of several caves in the vicinity. GB Cave is also nearby, which boasts the largest underground chamber in the Mendips. All the Mendip caves, though, apart from the show caves at Wookey and Cheddar, need special equipment and knowledge to explore. They're kept locked and you need special permission (and often a key) to go in.

Just on the other side of Tynings Farm the track curves sharply around to the right to join a road. On your left at this point is a gate, and beyond the gate a broad track running uphill straight across a field. Take this track, heading for the trees on the skyline a quarter of a mile away. Interestingly, the scenery changes dramatically when you reach them. On the downhill side of the gate is gentle, rolling farmland, on the other is the bare, windswept moor of Black Down, which is covered by gorse and coarse grass.

Once through the gate, don't take the track leading straight ahead – this cuts straight across Black Down and misses out much of the scenery. Instead, take the one on the right which starts off following the line of trees and then takes you across Black Down towards the top of Burrington Combe. The tracks across Black Down can be just as muddy as those in Rowberrow Warren, but at least the colour is different!

Believe it or not, concrete pillars were built on this hilltop during the Second World War, just in case the enemy tried to land aircraft here! Hard to imagine, since Black Down is, for most of the year, a sodden bog covered in extremely prickly vegetation.

On a clear day the views as you cross Black Down can be spectacular. With Tynings Farm about a mile behind you the triangulation pillar at the Down's highest point (Beacon Batch) should come into sight. Black Down is criss-crossed with tracks, so it can be difficult staying on the right one. Aim to keep the triangulation pillar a little way to your right as you pass it. From here the track begins to head downhill. Ahead of you is an excellent view of Blagdon lake, while to the left you'll see the gorse-studded slopes above Burrington Combe, Cheddar Gorge's less spectacular but still picturesque cousin. You're aiming to join the Combe near its upper end and then walk down parallel with it as it cuts a swathe through the hillside.

Keep following the track downhill for another half mile or so, with Blagdon lake still ahead of you. As you walk, you'll see drawing closer on your left the line of trees which marks the boundary of Black Down. When you come to a narrow track running off to the left and down to this line of trees, take it.

When you reach the trees, head back to the left, skirting the edge of Burrington Combe, and heading towards the village of Burrington itself. This track gives you a view of the rolling mass of Black Down to your left and, within a mile, a glimpse of the deep gash of the Combe to your right. Soon after this point the track splits into two. The route to the right takes you down into the Combe. The track leading left – which is the one you want – leads you down through a wood to a stream. Cross this stream, heading upwards and to the right. And, er... look out for some more mud here.

You soon emerge from amongst the trees and find yourself once more skirting Burrington Combe. Keep on this path, crossing a small babbling brook in the process. You get more views of Burrington Combe and the vegetation changes back to the open bracken of Black Down. The track now leads away from the Combe, however, and towards Mendip Lodge wood (ignore the smaller track running off to the right towards the Combe).

Keep walking towards the trees, even when you meet a crossroads, where broad paths converge from the left and right. The path now curves slightly to run alongside Mendip Lodge wood (to your right). You're now heading back towards Rowberrow Warren forest. There's more mud here, I'm afraid. You leave Black Down behind you for good now, as you head gently downhill through woodland. When you come to a minor meeting of ways, just head straight across.

By now you have the dense conifers of Rowberrow Warren on your left. Keep walking along the edge of the forest. You're aiming to skirt the northern edge of the forest, just cutting through at the last minute to reach The Swan. You'll soon see a gate and a track leading into the forest. This is the direction you want to go in, but not just yet. Look out instead for a second gate in about half a mile. This will take you back into the forest in the direction of the Swan.

From here, things can get a little tricky. Rowberrow Warren is riddled with tracks, most of which end up going in a different direction to the one you expect. You'll shortly come to a crossroads. Don't be tempted to head straight across, in what appears to be the right direction for the Swan. Instead, take a right. This takes you up and out of the forest. When you reach a signpost carry on straight ahead and slightly to the right. You then emerge above the valley at the bottom of School Lane. Cross the stream at the bottom then head off right, up School Lane and back to the Swan.

The Swan

The Swan is well off the beaten track, so you don't see too many tourists here. However, it's well known and popular amongst the locals, with its large, open interior which is nevertheless warm and cosy in the winter.

The Swan, Rowberrow. A cosy, warm atmosphere in winter, and plenty of parking!

The public bar is the largest part, and can hold perhaps three dozen people. The lounge area is a bit more comfortably furnished, and you could get a couple of dozen in here too before it started getting crowded.

There's not a huge range of beers, but what there is, is good, including Bass (probably the finest draught beer ever brewed), Butcombe (probably the most variable) and Wadworths 6X. I was once a 6X fan, but properly handled Bass has it beaten, I reckon. There's often a 'guest' beer too.

The bar food menu is good, with plenty of choice, but don't expect any bargains. But then it's a decent pub with lots of character in a rural location. The food's hot, the pub's warm and that's what counts after a long walk over Black Down.

There's a good-sized car park alongside the pub, and a huge parking area opposite. No problems here. Children, however, aren't really encouraged at night, but lunchtimes are OK, provided they stay in the lounge area.

Burrington Ham

Route: Rickford – Burrington – Burrington Combe – Burrington

Distance: 4 miles

Start: The Plume of Feathers, Rickford (ST 487593)

By car: Take the A371 out of Weston-super-Mare, turning left on to the A368 when you get to Banwell. Drive through Sandford to Churchill then head straight across when you get to the traffic lights. The A368 now winds eastwards for two miles, then turns sharp right and downhill into a tree-lined valley. Look out for a turn-off to the left and the Plume of Feathers nestling below the road to your left. (This left hand turning is very sharp – you need to swing out wide to make it in one.) There is some roadside parking, but you'd be well advised to get there while it's still quiet.

The Walk

This route takes you through the tiny but charming hamlet of Rickford, which has a stream running through its centre. From here you walk to Burrington Combe and then up and on to Burrington Ham which offers splendid views of Burrington Combe and Black Down.

Burrington Combe is like a poorer cousin to Cheddar Gorge. The cliffs are nowhere near as high and nowhere near as sheer. But then there isn't Cheddar Gorge's sprawling ghetto of souvenir shops and coffee houses, either. By any standards Burrington Combe is a pleasant little valley, and well worth a visit.

The going underfoot is good for the most part. Navigation along the edge of Burrington Ham can be tricky here and there, but the toughest part of the walk is undoubtedly the extremely stiff little climb at 'Aveline's Hole'. This is guaranteed to test both the legs and the lungs!

map 1

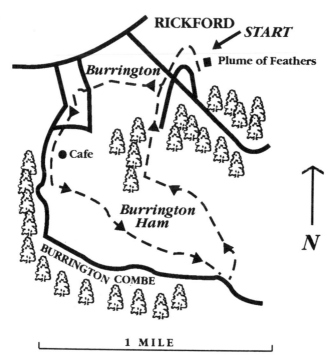

From the Plume of Feathers, head north (right) through the village. Incidentally, although the maps shows a road going all the way through, this route is actually impassable for motor vehicles – unless they're amphibious!

The road leads alongside a pretty little brook before turning sharp left to go over a bridge and then up to the main road. Facing you is a road leading away uphill, but if you look just to the right of this you'll see another, smaller, track (Burrington Lane) heading in the same direction. This is the one you want.

This path takes you along a metalled footpath into Burrington Village. You emerge with the village church in view – this is what you're aiming for. When you get there, walk through the gate into the churchyard, and then to the right of the church, looking out for a gate in the wall to your right. Go through the gate then turn left and then look for a gate, again on the left, leading on to a small playing field. Walk diagonally across to the gate in the opposite corner, then head diagonally across the next field in the same direction to a gate which opens out on to the road leading up Burrington Combe.

From here, walk up the Combe, looking out for a garden centre and pub on your left. The pub has a large gravel car park, and the path we want leads upwards to the left from this car park (just past the public toilets).

The climb at Aveline's Hole is very steep, and very rocky – a nasty, sharp little climb, though it does give you some nice views down into the Combe whenever you stop to rest. Before long, the path enters a wood, and you know that the worst is over. As the path levels out and you near the end of the climb, look out for a footpath leading off between the trees to the right. This will take you along the side of Burrington Ham, parallel with the Combe.

This path twists and turns a little and can be hard to follow at times. If you meet a fork in the track, go right, although there are few real opportunities for confusion. Periodically, the path breaks through the trees into a small opening, giving you spectacular views across to Black Down and down into Burrington Combe.

After a quarter of a mile or so, the path comes out on to more open ground. You're at the highest point of Burrington Ham now, and should soon come across a small, rocky ridge. On the other side of this ridge you'll see a path leading off to the left and downhill (east). Follow this track for half a mile. It twists and turns a little, even heading back uphill for a short distance before heading downhill again, to a layby alongside the road as it emerges from Burrington Combe. During the daytime there's nearly always an ice cream van parked here.

From this layby, look for a narrow track heading up through the trees a few yards from where you emerged. This leads you gently uphill in a northerly direction, heading across Burrington Ham back towards Burrington. Pretty soon the track is heading downhill again, descending finally into a conifer plantation where it turns 90 degrees to the right. A little further on it joins a road which leads between some houses back down to the A368, just opposite Rickford.

Rickford is a charming little village on a stream, just off the main Bath road.

All you have to do now is cross the road and wearily retrace your steps to the Plume of Feathers, wondering what on earth the author thought he was doing by introducing that climb up out of Burrington Combe.

The Plume of Feathers, Rickford. A good 'adventurous' menu, and lots of character.

The Plume of Feathers

The Plume of Feathers is a bit of a regulars pub. The bar faces you as you walk in, and as likely as not you'll have to weave your way between half a dozen jolly (and resident) revellers on bar stools to get served.

It's a very attractive little pub, though. The interior forms one long bar, so there are no separate public and lounge areas – although to the far left is a dartboard and pool table, while the area to the right is laid out for eating.

Beer choice is a tad disappointing for such a promising country pub. Ushers Best, Courage Best and Founders is now proving a familiar line-up. Founders is by far the best bet, unless you have a powerful thirst and no taste buds. Both the Ushers and Courage beers can be intoxicating, but only when consumed in vast quantities.

If the beer choice is limited, the same can't be said of the menu. Light eaters can choose from a range of jacket potatoes, starters and other snacks, while more adventurous gourmets get the chance to sample dishes like 'Venison in Pears, Juniper Berries and Red Wine'. The menu won't break the bank, but it's not cheap either.

Some of the pubs on the Mendips are clearly for the 'old folk' – nice, quiet, respectable and tasteful. The Plume of Feathers is a bit 'younger', with lots going on and lots of character. The only fly in the ointment is the car parking – or lack of it. The only place to leave your vehicle is on the road outside, next to the small river. Or, if you make even a small error, *in* the river!

Cheddar Gorge

Route: Cheddar – Cheddar Gorge – Black Rock – Long Wood – Charterhouse Farm – Cheddar Cliffs

Distance: 6 miles

Start: The Galleries Inn, Cheddar Gorge (ST 463538)

By car: From Wells, take the A371 north west, through Westbury-sub-Mendip, Rodney Stoke and Draycott to Cheddar. After a straight section running through the western outskirts of the village, the main road bears to the left. Take a right turn here and the road will lead you to a T-junction at the base of the Gorge. There is a reasonably-priced pay-and-display car park just to the right. Alternatively, there's rather less reasonably-priced all-day parking amongst the shops opposite the museum and at various sites all the way up the gorge.

The Walk

Cheddar is famous for three things: the cheese, the caves and the gorge – probably in that order. The cheese part is a bit of a nonsense, since cheese-making in Cheddar only dates back to the sixteenth century, while cheese has been manufactured in Somerset since 1170. There's also evidence that cheese made in Cheddar at the end of the eighteenth century was being sold elsewhere as 'Double Gloucester'. To cap it all, you can now buy 'Irish' cheddar, 'Canadian' cheddar and 'Australian' cheddar! To be fair, it's hardly one of the world's most memorable cheeses, even if it is one of the most popular.

The Cheddar caves are quite spectacular, true, but nowhere near as spectacular as those at Wookey.

Really, the true attraction of Cheddar is its sheer limestone cliffs. The cliffs reach a height of 450 feet in places and give tourists lots to gasp at, climbers lots to fall off and walkers lots to peer unsteadily over.

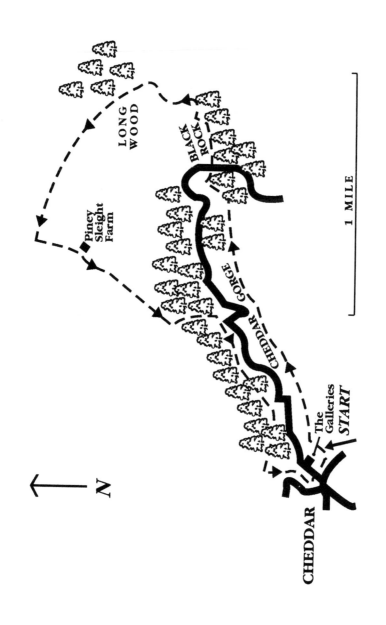

The sides of the gorge are far too sheer to have been formed by a river, or by glacial erosion. Current theory is that the gorge was formed by a river, but not a *surface* river. Instead, it's believed that a very large underground river gradually created a tunnel through the limestone far beneath the surface of the hills, and that the roof of this tunnel eventually collapsed into the river. There are many underground rivers in these limestone hills.

Cheddar Gorge is one of the most spectacular sights on the Mendips.

Cheddar Gorge is one of the most famous and popular tourist attractions of the Mendips. The name may derive from the Celtic words 'ced' ('cliff' or 'height') and 'dwr' (possibly meaning 'water'). There's no real evidence of occupation earlier than the ninth century, making the site a comparatively 'young' settlement.

The village itself can get uncomfortably crowded at the peak of the holiday season, but this walk quickly by-passes the tourist traps, since few stray more than a few hundred yards away from places you can park a car.

The walk leads along the sheer cliff-tops on the south-western side of the Gorge, before winding through Black Rock and Long Wood on to the top of the Mendips. From here you descend back down the Gorge on the other side. This stretch includes one of the most spectacular views in this part of the country...

The walking isn't arduous, but you do have to gain quite a lot of height on the way up. And the paths back down into Cheddar are rocky and can be slippery when damp.

Starting from the Galleries Inn, head back down the road to the museum on the corner, then turn left to walk up the narrow road alongside it. Within a hundred yards you'll see a flight of steps heading uphill to the left, amongst the houses. Follow this footpath up and then to the right. It soon joins a narrow road heading uphill and to the left again. As you near an iron gate, which blocks your path, look out for a stony track leading up through the trees to your left.

This path leads you up to a broader track. You emerge on to this track opposite a long flight of steps leading up from the Gorge – Jacob's Ladder. To your left is an observation tower which is well worth a quick detour, since the views from the top are excellent. Meanwhile, the route up the Gorge is to the right.

Keep following this track and you soon arrive at a gate and stile. Climb over and carry on. Just a little further on you reach a point where you have to be quite careful. After walking between a few trees you emerge on to a wide clearing. Just ahead and to your left is a slope leading up to a vantage point over the gorge. Directly ahead, the path appears to curve round slightly to the right and then carry on up the Gorge. Don't go this way! Instead, aim half way between these routes. As you get nearer to a gap in the vegetation, you'll see a red-tipped post poking out from the bracken. You must take the route to the LEFT of this post. (If you don't, no great harm is done, but you miss the cliff views and you will have to detour later on to rejoin the walk).

From here, just follow the track along the cliff edge. This section is likely to take you some time, not because it's especially long or arduous but because I guarantee you will be stopping frequently to admire the breathtaking views over the Gorge and the surrounding countryside. Be careful, because it's a long way down!

The whole of Cheddar Gorge is scarcely more than a mile long, and soon you reach the highest point of the cliff walk. Here you'll see a small stile and, once on the other side, look out for a track leading away to the left and downhill. This is the path down to Black Rock. It winds its way first of all through thick bracken and then, a little further on, through trees. The path gets a bit rocky and steep here, but presents no real problem with the right footwear. This section ends when you arrive at the main road as it emerges from the Gorge. Facing you across the road is a gate leading to Black Rock.

Cross straight over to the layby facing you and through the gate on to a broad footpath which winds its way past a disused quarry (Black Rock Quarry) before curving to the right towards Long Wood. Limestone was mined here, and the remains of a lime kiln can still be seen near the quarry.

As you approach the wood you'll see a gate ahead of you. Our route, however, curves round to the left here – you don't go through the gate. A little way ahead you'll see another, smaller, gate and a stile. Climb over the stile and take the track that leads uphill and slightly to the left.

This path takes you on a gentle climb through Long Wood. Soon, after another stile, you emerge on to open ground again. Walk on, keeping the hedgerow to your left, for about half a mile. (You'll pass a couple of stiles where there aren't any fences – very odd!)

Half a mile from Long Wood you'll come to a track which crosses your path from left to right. Go left. You now head gently downhill towards Piney Sleight Farm. As you reach the farm buildings, don't be tempted to follow the track round to the left. Instead, carry on through a gateway and past the farmhouse. Climb over another stile, and then follow the (rather faint) track across the field beyond. (You crest a small rise, then head diagonally to your right towards a stone wall.) The path now follows the edge of the field, next to this wall, passing through a gate. Just after this, you round a corner in the stone wall. Again, strike out diagonally towards the right-hand field edge, rejoining the wall again further on and going through another gate in the process. You soon arrive at another 'corner' in the wall. Again, strike out diagonally to your right, this time aiming for the corner of the field – and another stile.

Once over this final stile, look out for a track heading downhill to your left. Within 100 yards this joins a track heading downhill and to the right into Cheddar. A little further on, this track reveals an unexpected delight. The south-western cliffs are the most spectacular – so if you think about it you might expect to get the most spectacular views of them from the other (more gently sloping) side. Quite true. The path you're now following reaches a small clearing and you should spot a couple of foot-high wooden signposts in the ground ahead of you. One points to the left and is labelled, enigmatically, 'View'. The other points to the right and to 'Cheddar'.

The footpath to the 'View' is well worth the detour. It takes you a hundred yards out of your way, and it's steep, rocky and sometimes treacherous, but you get an amazing view of the Cheddar cliffs opposite that 999 out of 1000 tourists never see. It's a stunning sight.

From here, retrace your steps back to the clearing and pick up the route down into Cheddar. You now embark on a steep, twisting descent into the village (just keep following the signs). Cheddar is barely half a mile away, but this final stretch still seems to take an age. Finally you emerge on to a track which you follow downhill until it reaches a narrow road. Turn left here, still heading downhill, and left again when you reach a T-junction. within a couple of hundred yards, this road brings you out at the base of the Gorge. The Galleries Inn is 150 yards away to your left.

The Galleries Inn

The Galleries Inn is bang in the middle of Cheddar Gorge's main drag. So you'd expect it to be a cheap and cheerful tourists' pub selling nothing but keg beer and chips.

Wrong. The moment you walk in the door you know you're in for something different. Ahead of you is the bar, to the right an eating area, to the left a lounge area and beyond that a games room. The lighting is bright and cheery, the decor clean and tasteful and the piped music is actually decent for once.

The Galleries Inn, Cheddar Gorge. A bright atmosphere, great beers and a superb menu (and great value).

It's also a great place to sample a few odd brews. These include Boddington's (a pale, rather good brew from Up North) and a beer called 'Hobgoblin', which I would have loved to have tried but unfortunately on the night I dropped in it was 'off'.

The beer's not the only good thing about the place – the menu is pretty spectacular too. And not least because of the variety of dishes (including a variety of ploughman's' lunches, 'doorstops' and hot meals) but because of the value too. For example, there are a range of pasta dishes on offer at under £3. It's also a great place for vegetarians.

Apart from the menu, there's also a specials board, including tempting items like Fish Chowder. (Well, not tempting to everyone, perhaps, but to me it was.)

If it's the height of summer and you don't want to be indoors, there's ample seating outside, both on a patch of grass below the windows of the bar (the pub is built on a slope) or on a concrete verandah overlooking the Gorge's main street.

Parking is a bit of a nightmare in Cheddar Gorge, though. There's limited roadside parking, plus some roadside car parks at various points in the Gorge (you're charged a hefty whack to use them, though). There's also a moderately large pay-and-display car park at the bottom of the Gorge. If things are really bad, try the Park-and-Ride service (operates only during the tourist season, but then that's when the main problems are anyway).

The Galleries is definitely a 'young' pub, but it's very comfortable, the beer's good, the food's great (and great value) – one of the best pubs on the Mendips. It also happens to be at the centre of possibly the best walking on the Mendips.

STOP PRESS!! As this book went to press, The Galleries Inn had been put up for sale. Let's hope it is re-opened soon!

Around Priddy

Route: Priddy – St. Cuthbert's Swallet – North Hill – Priddy Nine Barrows

Distance: 5 miles

Start: The New Inn, Priddy (ST 527510)

By car: Priddy is probably most easily reached via the roads leading up through Cheddar Gorge and Burrington Combe. Once you reach the top of the Mendips, the village is well-signposted. The New Inn has a moderately large car park, and nearby is a large grassy area alongside a row of trees also given over to parking.

The Walk

Priddy is famous among historians for its Roman lead mines, its Iron Age 'barrows' and its medieval legacy – an annual sheep fair. However, it is, as far as I'm concerned, a rather grim little farming community with nothing to recommend it. However, since it's in such an interesting area, it's an ideal base for exploration.

Priddy lies at a height of 800 feet, in a shallow hollow right on top of the Mendip plateau. The name probably comes from the Welsh 'pridd' ('soil'). Visit after prolonged rain, and you'll wonder what the Welsh word for 'mud' is.

Arguably the most fascinating thing about the area is the profusion of burial mounds, or 'barrows', scattered around the fields. The most celebrated are the 'Priddy Nine Barrows' which sit in a line on the northern slopes of North Hill. (Strange, I've only ever counted eight...) These date back to 2000-700BC and are considered the finest examples in the country.

Priddy is at the centre of the Mendip 'plateau', an isolated farming area.

In addition, the area was an important lead mining centre in times gone by, and there's still plenty of evidence in the landscape to point to the scale of this industry. The Romans started it all and, although they principally mined the metal at Charterhouse, there's now evidence that they started workings at Priddy, too – note the Mineries Pond and the 'gruffy ground' at St. Cuthbert's Swallet created by surface digging. (Most of the visible evidence of mining, however, comes from later working, right up until the nineteenth century.)

The annual sheep fair (which is now more to do with fairs than sheep) has been held here ever since the Middle Ages, an era when the Black Death was a bigger threat to the European community than the ERM. Priddy was thought to be a 'healthier' spot than the lowlands. The thatched 'hurdles' in the middle of Priddy Green are of the type used at the time.

Priddy is also well-frequented by pot-holers, thanks to the presence nearby of Swildon's Hole. This underground maze is five miles long and descends to about 550 feet. It's one of the most popular caves on the Mendips.

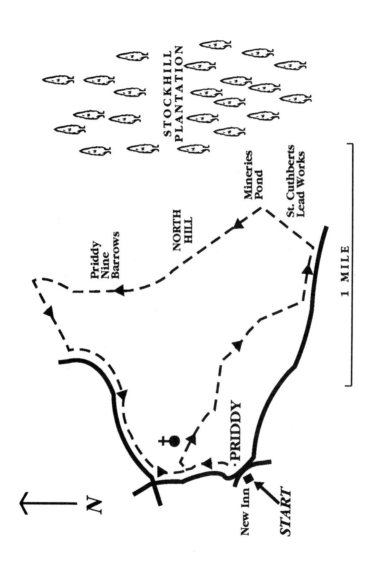

From the New Inn, head uphill (north) along the road towards Priddy church. A track leads up to the right from the road, then round towards the church. Keep following the lane, with the church now on your left and a couple of small buildings on your right, to a stile leading out on to the fields.

The footpath arrow on the stile points you down the slope to a stone wall at the bottom, where you turn left to head to the corner of the field and another stile. (You want the one right in the corner, not the unmarked stone stile facing you at first.) The wooden stile has an arrow pointing you diagonally uphill towards the left, but before you can start the climb you have to negotiate a second, stone, stile.

Now then, this is the tricky bit. You must aim uphill, rather to the left of hedgerow at the top of the slope. Once past this, head for the far left-hand corner of the field. You'll see a gate just before the corner, on your left, but you actually want a stone stile a few yards to the right of this (it's so ancient it's almost invisible – if you didn't know it was there you would miss it completely).

From here, walk along the left-hand edge of the field beyond, going through a gap in the stone wall ahead and then bear to the right and downhill towards another stone wall enclosing a small field. Now according to the map, the footpath goes over this wall and then follows the left edge of the field. Do this (being careful not to damage the wall) and you will arrive at what looks like an *ad hoc* camp-site which, according to the map, you should be able to walk through. You can't, because it's securely fenced off. What you can do is climb over the barbed wire fence separating you from a track on your left, and proceed from there.

Farmers and landowners are not known for their willingness to accommodate walkers. Fortunately, provided you stick to the paths defined, the law will always come down on your side – even to the extent that you can demolish obstructions preventing you from using a public right of way.

That little bit of unpleasantness over, you follow this track all the way down to the road running east out of Priddy. Follow this road east past some houses and a right-hand kink in the road, and then look out for a turning off to the left to Underbarrow Farm.

Curiously, you can't stay on this track as it curves round to the right but must instead walk through a small car park and, beyond that, what looks like an unkempt back yard, to a stile in the far right-hand corner. Climb over this stile, cross the track and then climb over another stile before bearing left to head towards the Mineries Pond.

Over to the right now you can make out the uneven 'gruffy' ground of St. Cuthbert's lead works, founded by the Romans and mined, intermittently, ever since.

At the Mineries Pond you'll see a small notice set into the ground telling you a bit about this area, which actually forms part of a 123-acre reserve. It's been designated a Site of Special Scientific Interest because of its 'invertebrate interest' and 'the heath and bog vegetation'. Interestingly, you won't see any animals grazing in the reserve – this is due to the high lead concentrations in the ground. Botanists should, apparently, look out for Spring Sandwort, Sea Campion, Marsh and Spotted Orchis, Purple Moor Grass and various ferns and lichens.

The notice also refers to 'buddle pits'. These were washing pits used in the lead manufacturing process and caused a bit of a fuss in the mid-late nineteenth century. The proprietors of the paper mill at Wookey Hole reckoned that they were getting contaminated water from the Priddy buddle pits. After court proceedings, the Priddy mines were forced to clean up their acts. They finally closed down in the early part of the twentieth century (one of the last of the region's mines to do so).

Now you have to be a bit careful here. The main route heads north east towards a major forestry plantation, but we want to go uphill to the left, following the left hand edge of the field. You climb gradually to the top of North Hill, negotiating a stile to head on towards a small building on the skyline.

Once over the crest of the hill you keep to the left of the field and descend towards a gate in the fence facing you. (There ought to be a route through this fence slightly to the right, but there isn't, so you have to climb this gate.)

You're now in amongst the Priddy Barrows. They're impressive more for their known age and significance rather than their appearance. Walk to the right of the first two, just beyond the fence, then cut across downhill to walk through the centre of the line of eight facing you. Then you carry on downhill towards the gate facing you in the corner of the field (look for the narrow gap between the trees). Here you've got a choice. If you're sick of kicking your way through long grass you can go through the gate to the road and an easy walk back to Priddy. If not, you can save a bit of time by turning to your left then striking out diagonally across the field, aiming somewhat to the left of the tree poking above the skyline on its own. If your aim is good you will arrive at a gate on to the road on the other side. From here, it's a simple walk of about a mile along country lanes back to Priddy.

The New Inn

Well, Priddy may be a grim little farming community high on the Mendips, but the New Inn is altogether much more welcoming. It's obvious that people come from miles around for the food, and probably the atmosphere too.

The New Inn is a low, sprawling building next to the village green. It started life back in the fifteenth century as a farmhouse but was later turned into an ale-house, presumably to serve to local lead miners. The pub underwent a major refurbishment in the 1970s. Outhouses were converted into bars, a skittle alley and conservatory were added and bedrooms for guests built upstairs. The result is an excellent country pub.

Once inside you can either go left into the public bar (bright and lively) or go right into the lounge/eating area. The lounge features a large fireplace and is separated into two main areas. The second leads out to the conservatory at the back of the pub (which is where you take kids).

The beer choice is pretty good, consisting of Wadworths' 6X (good), Marstons' Pedigree (good) and 'Hardys' (who?). The main attraction, though, is the menu. 'Snacks and Appetisers' include soup, whitebait and paté, and to follow there are omelettes, trout, lamb, steaks and various vegetarian dishes. Jacket spud fans can choose from half a dozen different fillings. Oh, and there's a daily list of specials. Prices aren't cheap, but they're not unreasonable, either.

The New Inn is one of the best Mendip pubs. It's bright and lively, and offers good beer and food in excellent surroundings. It's a great way of combining a brisk walk with a good evening meal.

Parking is no problem at all. There's a medium-sized gravel parking area right outside the pub, but you can park alongside the village green too. Unless you plan to use the (stone-floored) public bar, though, leave those muddy walking shoes in the car.

The New Inn, Priddy. A good menu, cosy bars and a busy,
friendly atmosphere.

Stockhill Plantation

Route: Castle of Comfort – Stockhill

Distance: 2-4 miles

Start: Castle of Comfort Inn (ST 544532)

By car: From Wells, take the A39 north east, taking a left turn at Green Ore along the B3135, then turning right at the crossroads about two miles further on. The Castle of Comfort is on the left about half a mile later, as the road bends round to the left. There is a large parking area outside.

The Walk

This is the only walk in the book without a clear-cut route. This is because it's very difficult to specify one! Like Rowberrow Warren, to the west, Stockhill is a Forestry Commission plantation, mostly coniferous. It's also open to the public and is criss-crossed with tracks and lanes. So much so, that a good sense of direction will stand you in much better stead than any directions I could offer.

The Castle of Comfort is the nearest pub. (Actually, the Hunters Lodge Inn is nearer, but rather less amenable.) From the pub car park, you're faced with a walk of no more than half a mile along roads to the plantation. A set of crossroads marks the nearest corner of the plantation, and you can go either left or straight on here – there are entrances into the plantation along both roads. I'd recommend going straight on.

If you don't fancy walking down to the plantation from the pub, there is a picnic area half way down the western edge of the forest. You can drive in here – there's plenty of parking, thanks to a number of small parking areas alongside a circular track running a little way into the forest and then back to the road.

The Stockhill Plantation near Priddy is nearly as large as Rowberrow Warren.

map 21

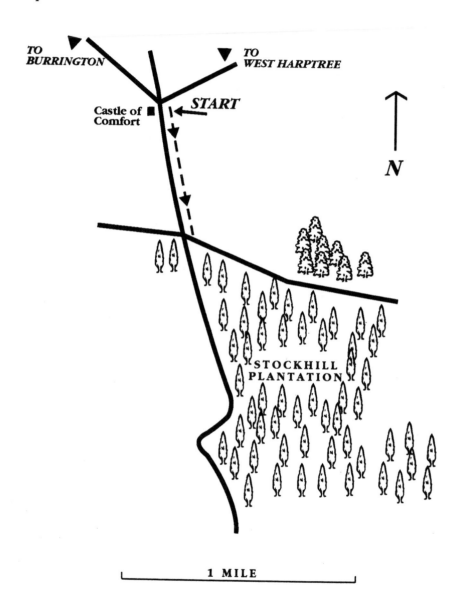

1 MILE

Rowberrow Warren is the more attractive and varied forest, I think – Stockhill has no babbling brooks to walk alongside and no great changes in height – but Stockhill enjoys the more exposed position, right on top of the Mendip plateau. From the road down the western side, you also get excellent views of the barren North Hill and the famous Priddy Barrows. A footpath leads across to the abandoned Roman lead mines at St. Cuthberts, to the south west, if you fancy a diversion.

As I say, there are so many tracks and paths through the Stockhill Plantation that it's impossible to pick a route. Instead, it's much more pleasant just to spend an hour or so walking the lanes – you could just as easily be deep in a forest in the American Rockies, as in an artificial forestry plantation on the Mendips.

If you're feeling adventurous, you could try the footpath leading from the north-eastern corner of the plantation north to West End, then west across the fields to the Castle of Comfort. Navigating across fields on the Mendip plateau, however, is not a terribly rewarding occupation.

There's only one thing to watch out for with this plantation – mud. The Rowberrow Warren plantation is muddy, but this one is muddier. Wear proper boots or wellingtons if the weather is bad, and expect to have to dodge some extensive quagmires on the bridleways. (A change of footwear for the pub is essential except in the driest conditions.)

The Castle of Comfort

The Castle of Comfort is no castle, but it is pretty comfortable. You walk through the doors into a larger than average public bar with a dartboard over on the far right and enough seating for a couple of dozen people.

Public bar it may be, but it's still comfortable and nicely decorated. For those who fancy a bit more style, though, there's a lounge to the left, and seating for a coachload of people. Generally, the place is not overloaded with character, but is still one of the better pubs on the Mendips – certainly in this area.

Beer drinkers can choose from Butcombe (seldom inspiring, often dubious), Founders (heavy, but good) and Bass (a wonderful beer, treated properly).

The Castle of Comfort, near Priddy. Lots of room, a good menu and no shortage of parking.

The menu is pretty extensive. It includes lots of snacks, salads and quiche-type dishes for those fed up of chips with everything. Or you can try a steak, or such exotica as Pork a la Creme or Baggage Trout. Prices are pretty reasonable considering the choice and type of dish.

Children under 14 have to stay in the garden. No great hardship in good weather, since there is ample seating and things to play on. The garden is to the rear, alongside the huge car park.

There is no doubt a small local contingent of regulars, but for the most part the Castle of Comfort is a pub for visitors, or those who want an evening meal out. It's not too formal, though, so as long as you don't tramp in wearing battledress and walking boots, you're unlikely to attract attention.

Westbury Beacon

Route: Rodney Stoke – Hill Lane – hill fort – Westbury Beacon – Westbury Quarry

Distance: 6 miles

Start: The Rodney Stoke Inn, Rodney Stoke (ST 484503)

By car: From Wells, take the A371 north west (the Cheddar Road). Rodney Stoke is about 4-5 miles along this road, and the Rodney Stoke Inn is on your left as you drive through the village. There's a substantial car park to the side of the pub. There may be some roadside parking nearby, but you'll have trouble finding any.

The Walk

Rodney Stoke is one of the several picturesque little villages nestling at the base of the southern Mendip slopes between Cheddar and Wells. From here, though, it's only a short (but sharp!) climb up on to the wide open expanses of the Mendip plateau. These not only give you a taste of hilltop walking, but some great views across the country to the south.

From the Rodney Stoke Inn, head straight across the road up the lane facing you (Hill Lane). This is marked as a 'No Through Road', but for the time being it's a well-surfaced lane. Are you feeling fit, though? You'll need to be, because you'll be climbing around 700 feet over the next half mile or so!

Hill Lane soon gets very steep indeed. It's just as well, then, that you can turn to take in the excellent views behind you every time you stop to rest. To the south and west is the line of hills between Wookey and Wedmore, while beyond Wookey you can see the distinctive shape of Glastonbury Tor.

Hill Lane soon curves round to the left, by which time the worst is largely over. There's still plenty of climbing left to do yet, though. You soon pass Rodney Stoke Vineyard on your left, and from here on, Hill Lane slowly deteriorates into a rocky track.

The wide open skies of the Mendip plateau are only a short (stiff) walk up from Rodney Stoke.

You carry on climbing, starting to bear round to the right and up the hill again. Hill Lane finally ends in a gate leading out on to open hillside. Now, directly ahead of you, you'll see a small, derelict stone building. Once through the gate, walk to the right of this building, then curve round to the left as you walk uphill towards the stone wall ahead of you. From this hillside, incidentally, the views are breathtaking. You can see right across the Somerset flatlands, from Wedmore to the south, to the isolated summit of Brent Knoll even as far as Brean Down and the island of Steep Holm in the Bristol Channel. To the west you can also see the line of the Mendip hills, all the way from their seaward end.

Still climbing, you see two gateways ahead of you. Aim 50-100 yards to the left of these, looking for a stile over the wall. When you reach it, head straight across the field beyond to another stile in the wall facing you. Once over this, head west to meet the right-hand wall of the field on the other side, following it as it heads towards an isolated clump of trees.

As you walk this section, you're passing, to your right on the other side of the wall, the site of an Iron Age settlement, one of scores on the

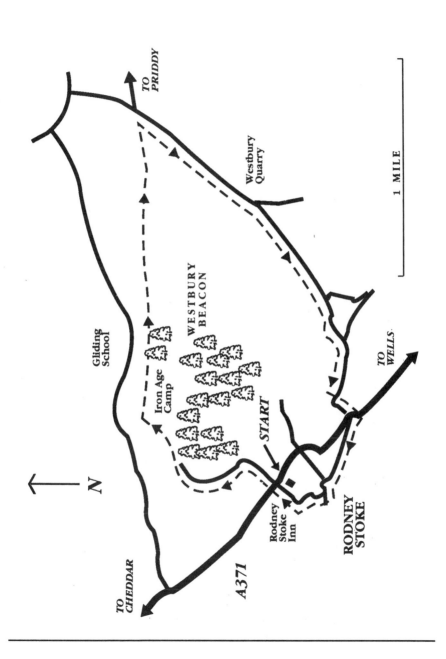

Mendips, inhabited from 700BC. To the left is Halesland Airfield, used as a glider training school by the Air Training Corps. The gliders' wings sometimes give a high, whistling sound – an eerie effect when you don't know where the sound is coming from until you look up.

There's another stile in the corner of the field by the clump of trees ahead of you. Go over this and carry on more or less due east. From here you're heading gradually downhill towards the road, about a mile away, crossing another five fields in the process. Head straight across the first field, walk parallel with the wall on your right in the second, parallel with the wall on the left in the third and then in the fourth field, join up with the wall on the right. Keep to the right in the fifth field to emerge on to the road via a stile on the other side.

You go right here, following this road as it twists and turns downhill back towards Rodney Stoke. I usually avoid road routes, but I make an exception here because this road is usually very quiet and offers some excellent views. To begin with you take in the wide open spaces of the Mendip plateau and then, as you begin to descend, you get views far across the Somerset flatlands.

When you reach Westbury Quarry (on your left) the road ahead forks left and right. Take the right-hand fork (Broad Road). You now start descending more steeply, and after much twisting and turning and more picturesque views, Broad Lane finally emerges at the main Wells-Cheddar road. Instead of walking back to the Rodney Stoke Inn along this busy road, though, go straight across and do down the lane opposite. This heads downhill to the right, descending into Rodney Stoke village. Go left when you reach the T-junction, then right 50 yards further on. This picturesque little country lane now twists and turns back to the main road, finally emerging alongside the Rodney Stoke Inn.

The Rodney Stoke

There is a variety of attractive roadside pubs on the road between Cheddar and Wells. The Rodney Stoke is amongst the most picturesque. It's on the right-hand side if you're travelling in the Wells direction, and boasts an ample car park. Inside, there are two bars to choose from. The 'snug' bar at the front of the pub is a bit of a noisy locals' haunt. Not the sort of place you'd feel particularly comfortable as a stranger, but probably the best bet if you've just returned from a muddy hike.

The lounge bar is at the rear of the pub, and is altogether more genteel. There's a small sitting area next to the bar and behind that is a larger 'restaurant' section. The lounge bar also has a well in the middle of the floor! It's been fitted with a glass top and serves as a table, but it's still something of a curiosity...

Beer drinkers can choose from the ubiquitous and thoroughly drinkable draught Bass and draught Worthington Best (there's one you don't often see on draught). Diners have a much wider choice. Admittedly, it's pretty standard pub fare for the most part, consisting of various steaks, jacket potatoes, salads, snacks, starters and sweets. It's not especially cheap, either.

Never mind, though, because the lounge bar is very pleasant. You can take kids in, too, providing they're in the restaurant section (and sitting down). It's a nicely decorated, cosy country pub. It doesn't have a huge amount of atmosphere, but the parking's easy, the location's convenient and just about everyone is going to like it.

The Rodney Stoke Inn. An attractive, unusual lounge with a well in the centre.

Around Wells

The Walks

Around Wells   From The Crown Hotel, Wells (ST 551458)

Wookey Hills   From The Pheasant Inn, Wookey (ST 503453)

Ebbor Gorge   From The Wookey Hole Inn, Wookey Hole
                          (ST 533476)

Around North Wootton From The Crossways Inn, North Wootton
                          (ST 566416)

Glastonbury Tor   From The Waggon and Horses, Glastonbury
                          (ST 506403)

The Area

Wells is best known for its cathedral, but the Bishop's Palace just next door is equally fascinating. It's an ancient structure standing in extensive grounds surrounded by a high, castellated wall and even a moat.

The area around Wells is just as fascinating as the city itself. The village of Wookey, just to the west, is surrounded by small, low hills which offer some fascinating walking.

Wookey's 'sister' town, Wookey Hole, is even more fascinating. Tourists flock from all over the country to visit the spectacular Wookey Hole caves, but walkers should head for the little-known Ebbor Gorge, just half a mile to the north west. Although well served by paths, Ebbor Gorge is still only accessible to reasonably determined pedestrians. Those that make the effort find themselves in a miniature version of Cheddar Gorge, but without the traffic and without the gift shops. The climb out of Ebbor Gorge is a scramble up a rocky slope, and at the top you can look down on one of the most marvellous little spots in the Mendips.

To the east of Wells, the Mendips begin to lose their identity as the hills spread out into the surrounding countryside. But there are still many picturesque little areas to explore, one of which is the village of North Wooton, which boasts its own vineyards!

One landmark dominates the south-facing views everywhere you go, though – Glastonbury Tor. No visit to the area would be complete without a visit to this town, which was the source of Christianity in this country and home to one of its largest and most influential abbeys. It's also reckoned, some say, to be the home of King Arthur.

Wells

Route: Wells Cathedral – South View – King's Castle Wood – Tor Hill

Distance: 5 miles

Start: The Crown Hotel, Wells (ST 551458)

By car: Wells is pretty well equipped with car parks. There are a couple of reasonably-priced pay-and-display car parks within a stone's throw of the Cathedral and, if you get there early, you may get one of the parking spaces available in front of the Cathedral itself. The Crown Hotel has a small car park of its own.

The Walk

Wells is an interesting city to walk around in its own right. The Cathedral itself is the major tourist attraction, of course, but the Bishop's Palace, right next door, is equally fascinating. It dates back to the thirteenth century, with the gatehouse and drawbridge being added a century later – it's a celebrated example of its type.

Wells became a city in 1201, thanks to a royal charter granted by King John. Its importance in medieval times is demonstrated by the scale and grandeur of the cathedral. These days, it's just another provincial town, though (apart from its historical interest), yet it's still a good base from which to explore the Mendips.

The walk takes you through the grounds around the Bishop's Palace, then eastwards out of Wells to climb up into King's Castle Wood and then descend back down into Wells via Tor Hill. It's an excellent stretch for those who have had enough culture and just fancy a bit of fresh air...

The Crown Hotel is on the narrow street directly in front of the Cathedral entrance. However, it's not the Cathedral we want, but the entrance to the Bishop's Palace just to the right. It's a rather grand

The magnificent Wells Cathedral is one of the major tourist attractions of the area.

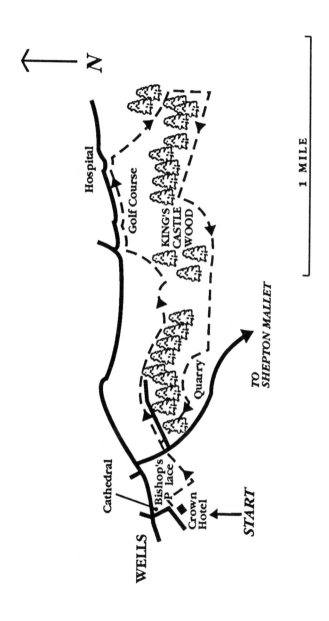

archway built into a turret in the wall around the grounds, and don't be put off by signs indicating the opening hours – these refer only to the Palace itself, not the grounds.

Go through the archway, then head to the right along the broad path next to the moat around the Palace. When you get to the corner of the moat up ahead, turn left and carry on alongside it.

Soon you reach the end, and the main road running south east out of Wells towards Shepton Mallet. Cross over the road, then carry on along the track facing you on the opposite side of the road. This is Torhill Lane, and it leads you past the lower edge of Tor Hill, a National Trust property.

Torhill Lane ends in a gate which leads on to open fields next to houses on your left. A track leads across the first field to another gate, and beyond this you should see it continuing across the next, larger, field, heading slightly to the right towards another gate. Beyond this gate is the Wells Golf Course, and rather stern notices insist you keep to the paths indicated. Discretion being the better part of valour, follow the arrow to the left, which brings you within a few yards to a track running alongside the houses next to the golf course. Follow this track as it winds its way along the edge of the golf course and finally emerges on to the main road at a junction.

Take the right turning, heading past the entrance to the golf club and as far as the turn-off (on your left) to the hospital. Here, on the right, you'll see a footpath sign pointing back across the golf course. Ignore this one. Instead, walk a few yards further up the road, looking out on your right for a metal gate and an unmarked stile alongside it.

Climb over this stile, then head downhill and to your left to a stile at the bottom of the field. Once over this stile, follow the hedge to your left as it curves round to the left, looking out for another stile at the bottom of the slope. Climb this stile, then head directly uphill to the gate facing you about thirty yards away. Once over that, head diagonally to the left uphill, aiming for the corner of a copse coming in from the left at the top of the slope. As you round the corner of this copse, strike out again across the open ground beyond, this time aiming for the leftmost corner of the next clump of trees. This is, in fact, the eastern margin of King's Castle Wood.

Follow the edge of the trees to a gate, then turn right to carry on following the edge of the wood. The route is fairly clear from now on. As the trees open out, you get good views across to the south towards Dulcote Hill.

As you near the looming, tree-shrouded hill ahead of you (and the remains of King's Castle), the track drops down to the right in amongst the trees. Within yards, though, you reach a branching of tracks. One route leads ahead and up towards King's Castle in the middle of the wood, while the route we want leads downwards and to the left, soon curving round to head west towards Wells, alongside the lower margin of the wood.

As you walk along this track you'll see a sign on your right telling you more about the wood. For example, that it stands on 'Carboniferous Clifton Down limestone'. By way of a diversion, you can go through the wood to the summit of the hill and the still-visible ramparts of an iron age fort.

That's enough to keep the archaeologists happy. Meanwhile, naturalists should look out for various interesting species of wild plant, including Small-leaved Lime, Solomon's Seal, Meadow Saffron, Wood Goldilocks and the Nettle-Leaved Bellflower. You might even spot an owl or a buzzard – maybe even a deer.

The path carries on to the western edge of the wood, where it joins a track heading back to Wells. When you arrive at a large house to the right of the track, look out for a path heading diagonally off to the right towards Strawberry Wood. When you reach the edge of the trees, go left. This route will soon curve to the right and emerge in the small clearing on top of Tor Hill. From here you descend back down to Torhill Lane and retrace your steps back past the Bishop's Palace to the Crown Hotel.

The Crown Hotel

You can't get a much better location than this! The Crown Hotel forms part of an ancient row of buildings on the main square in Wells, just in

*The Crown Hotel, Wells. A spacious interior with a nice atmosphere
and a good menu.*

front of the Bishop's Palace. There's also a restaurant here, as well as a bar (the Penn Bar and Eating House).

From the outside the place looks cramped an medieval, but inside, the bar is quite large. Ahead of you is an area with tables in front of a large fireplace. Beyond that is a food-serving area. To the right is the main bar area and beyond that, at the back of the building, a larger eating area (it's a bit plain and gloomy, though).

Curiously, on the night of our visit, we were told to go to the restaurant for food – it may be a good idea to call beforehand to check whether bar food is going to be available.

The Penn Bar is quite attractively decorated inside. It's quite posh, but not enough to make walkers uncomfortable. Leave your boots and anoraks in the car, though.

The beer choice is small, but good. Ruddles is always a good standby, and Directors is a quite a strong, heavy beer but still bitter. If you fancy something a bit more innocuous, there's also Yorkshire on draught.

Wells is good for tourist information, and there's a small noticeboard in the bar detailing the various current local attractions – a nice touch.

Parking in Wells can be troublesome, though it's not as bad as many other historical towns. If you arrive early enough, there should still be spaces in the main square (a fairly expensive pay-and-display park). Otherwise, use one of the larger pay-and-display parks near the centre and walk the rest of the way. This is a much cheaper, if less convenient, option.

Wookey Hills

Route: Yarley – Yarley Hill – Callow Hill – Castle Farm

Distance: 5 miles

Start: The Pheasant Inn, Wookey (ST 503453)

By car: From Wells, take the A371 towards Cheddar, turning left just on the outskirts of Wells to take the road to Wookey. The Pheasant Inn is on the left in about a mile, a few yards after a lane branches off to the left. (This lane forms part of the walk.) There's a good-sized car park alongside the pub.

The Walk

Most of this walk is on country roads (you can cut out the bridleway sections altogether if you wish). This won't please hardened hill-walkers but it's idea for families – all the more so because the landlord of the Pheasant positively encourages families (if only more publicans did!).

These roads, though, are narrow and very quiet, so traffic shouldn't be a problem. Neither will you need hosing down before you can go in the pub!

There are a few moderate hills to climb (nothing too severe, though) and lots of sights to take in along the way, including views across the Somerset levels towards Meare and a glimpse of the site of Fenny Castle, an ancient Saxon stronghold.

The Pheasant Inn straddles two roads – the main road west towards Wedmore and the narrow lane leading off south west over the hill. You leave the pub car park to follow this lane uphill.

After passing some cottages on your left you reach a red brick house at a crossroads. Bear right here, then turn right at the junction just beyond. This road is Hilliers Lane and it leads you first downhill and then up and to the left towards Yarley. Over to the right you can see across past Knowle Hill to the southern slopes of the Mendips.

As you drop down into Yarley, you join another road. Follow this road to the right, then at the next junction, a few yards further on, go left. A few yards up this hill you'll come to Keeping Cottage on the right. There's a public footpath through what looks like the cottage garden, to the right of the house.

At this point you've got a choice. You can either take this footpath, which leads out on to the top of Yarley Hill or, if you have a pushchair, or don't want to risk getting muddy, you can carry on up the hill and pick up the route again in about 400 yards.

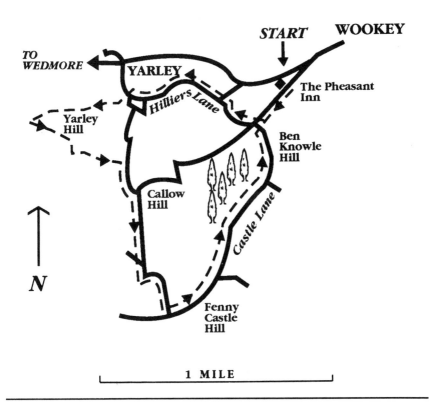

If you take the route on to the hill, you walk past Keeping Cottage, along a bridleway (via a couple of gates) until the end of the bridleway. Carry on uphill, across the field and up on to the top of the hill. From here you get some excellent all-round views on a clear day, principally of the Somerset flatlands to the south west – once used for the production of peat.

To the south you may be about to make out the site of the Abbot's Fish House at Meare. Back in the days when Glastonbury Abbey was at its height, the Abbey's own fishermen lived here, taking their catch from the large lake that existed here before the extensive drainage schemes that reclaimed the land. ('Meare' probably derives from 'mere', or 'lake'.)

From the top of Yarley Hill, head downwards, over the brow to the metal gate facing you. Go left on the other side, following the track – which becomes a bridleway. This takes you back to the road leading up out of Yarley.

Head up and over the rise, then downhill to a sharp left-hand bend in the road. Go right here, and head downhill. Ahead of you is Glastonbury Tor. After a fairly steep descent between high hedgerows the road takes a sharp left turn. On your left now you can see the slopes of Bower's Hill. Within a few yards the road turns sharp right again and then, about 200 yards later, you reach Ashmore Drove. Turn left here.

To your right now is a rather pleasant little stream. And across the field beyond the stream, you'll see a small hillock, with a couple of rather intoxicated-looking trees on the top. This is Fenny Castle, thought to be the site of a wooden Saxon stronghold.

The road gradually curves round to the north east, past Fenny Castle House on the right and then, a little further on, the remains of a stone cross opposite Castle Farm. You're now heading towards the 320-foot high Ben Knowle Hill. The road carries on north west to its base, then heads to the left and uphill.

After a short distance you arrive at a red brick house remarkably similar to the one you saw much earlier in the walk. So similar, in fact, that if you turn right at the crossroads here and head downhill you'll find yourself back at the Pheasant Inn.

All that remains of Fenny Castle, near Wookey, is a low mound covered in trees.

The Pheasant Inn

The Pheasant Inn is a pretty ordinary-looking pub, but inside you're due for a surprise. There is a small public bar (called 'The Dog Room') which you could just about cram a dozen people into. It's rough and ready in a deliberate kind of way and has lots of character. On Friday evenings you can sup your pint to the musical strains of a live Blues singer.

Most of the pub, though, is given over to a restaurant. And a restaurant, at that, with a very good menu.

Indeed, it seems that the road leading west from Wells through Wookey is known locally as 'The Food Run' because of the number of pubs serving gourmet-standard food. The Pheasant itself employs a French chef, and the current landlord is busy establishing its reputation as a high-quality eating house.

The restaurant won't win too many prizes for comfort, since most of the seats are upright wooden benches set right against the wall in the traditional fashion. The interior, though, is cosy and charming, which makes up for it. Another plus point is that children and families are welcome, even in the bar (where the locals know they have to mind their 'p's and 'q's).

The food choice consists of a menu of normal pub-style food, plus an a la carte menu for the more discerning palate. There are a couple of beers on draught to choose from, but you'd come here more for the food than the beer.

Car parking is good, with space for a couple of dozen cars. You can sit outside if you want to, but there's not too much to see apart from traffic.

Ebbor Gorge

Route: Wookey Hole – Ebbor Wood – Ebbor Gorge

Distance: 3 miles

Start: The Wookey Hole Inn, Wookey Hole (ST 533476)

By car: Wookey Hole is just a couple of miles to the north west of Wells and is easily reached by a variety of roads. It's well signposted. There is only one road through Wookey Hole, and the pub is on your right (travelling north), together with a modest car park facing it on the left-hand side. If this is full, the Wookey Hole Caves complex boasts a truly giant car park a little further up the road on your left.

The Walk

Wookey Hole is (justifiably) famous for its cave. If you've never seen it, it's definitely worth a visit, especially as new chambers are being opened up all the time. The current route passes through no fewer than 25 of them, but that's unlikely to be the final tally.

The cave was once home to Celtic people before the Roman invasion, incidentally. And also, we're told, to the Witch of Wookey, a fifteenth-century recluse, who was believed to have cast spells on the village folk. The story goes that she was finally turned to stone by holy water wielded by a young monk from Glastonbury, and that her remains can still be seen to this day. Certainly, if you peer hard enough at the wall of one of the chambers, your tour guide can eventually convince you that the witch's face is visible in the rock. If, that is, you squint in a certain sort of way out of one eye!

Wookey Hole is by no means the only cave in the area. The Mendips are riddled with them. Around Wookey Hole, Bronze Age bones, cooking utensils and other relics have been found in abundance, all left by cave-dwellers. Badger Hole shows signs of occupation 25,000 years ago – the Stone Age!

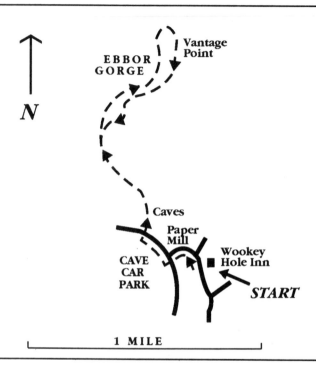

However, as far as the walker is concerned, Wookey Hole boasts another, largely unknown, attraction – Ebbor Gorge. The most famous 'gorge' in the area is, of course, the one at Cheddar. Ebbor Gorge is only a fraction of the size, but it is still a fascinating and spectacular sight. It's also situated away from the roads and is not packed with tourists, even at the height of the season. The Gorge and surrounding land were presented to the National Trust in 1967 in memory of Sir Winston Churchill, by Mrs Olive Hodgkinson (the Hodgkinson clan figures large in local history). Being a National Trust reserve, there are plenty of well-maintained, well-signposted paths.

From the pub, head north up the main street, following the road as it curves to the left and heading past the paper mill. This was Somerset's first paper mill, in fact, going back to the early seventeenth century and finally closing as recently as 1972 (machine-made paper had become too cheap, and the labour-intensive processes being used at the mill could no longer compete). The place is now a museum.

A little further on is the entrance to the cave. The road then curves around to the right again. Keep going, past a turning towards some riding stables on your right and past six cottages on your left. These cottages (collectively known as 'the Croft') were built at the start of this century for mill workers. Three of them are reckoned to be haunted! One periodically gives off a strange odour which terrifies animals, another echoes to the stomping of a crippled old lady up the wooden stairs and the third features the ghost of a white-haired old lady who died back in the '50s. She hasn't been seen since being exorcised by the Bishop of Bath and Wells; our pace quickens unaccountably as we pass this point, and soon we're looking out for a footpath on the right running past the side of a house – it's marked by a signpost.

Follow the track beyond as it curves to the left then heads across more open ground. You soon reach a gate, and a sign telling you a bit about Ebbor Gorge. Go through the gate, and carry on along the track.

This track now leads along the base of the valley through woodland. You shortly arrive at a meeting of tracks, and from here follow the signs to the Gorge.

You're soon climbing gently upwards into the Gorge, and the surrounding landscape grows more rugged and spectacular. Finally you emerge into the Gorge itself. It's much smaller than Cheddar Gorge, but every bit as sheer, confined and spectacular – and much quieter!

Oh, and look out for adders – especially during hot weather. These snakes are nowhere near as uncommon as most would like to think. Their bite is rarely fatal these days, but urgent medical attention is necessary should you be foolish enough to tempt one of them with a bit of bare leg.

Until now, the going has been very easy. But be warned – the climb out of the Gorge at its far end is steep and rocky. Only the comparatively infirm will have to resort to using their hands, but even the able-bodied will have to watch their step. The Gorge and this climb are one of the hidden jewels of the Mendips.

At the top of this rocky climb, the track carries on to another junction. Follow the signpost pointing right to the Car Park. A little further on, another car park signpost points to a track heading downhill to the left, while the track you're on carries on straight ahead. Where does it go?

The answer is soon revealed. It leads to a small clearing on the eastern cliff-tops above the Gorge. It gives you a superb view down into the Gorge itself and across to the south west.

This short walk to the cliff-tops is a detour, though. Once you've taken in the views, retrace your steps and take that route down to the car park. The track winds its way downhill through the trees – there are steps for the more treacherous sections. Keep your eyes peeled and you might just spot one of the deer than live in the woods. They're shy creatures, though, and usually stay well out of the way of humans.

You finally emerge just a few yards from the junction where you first followed the signpost to the gorge. From here it's simply a matter of heading back along the track to the road, and then descending back into Wookey Hole village.

The Wookey Hole Inn

When you step into this place, you're sadly in for a bit of a surprise. From the outside, the Wookey Hole Inn (also a hotel) looks like a grand Tudor-style hunting lodge. Once inside, you realise its best days are gone. It's nicely enough decorated (it must once have been quite posh), but it's now a tiny bit grubby and dilapidated. Still, it is the only pub in Wookey Hole, and it's recently been taken over by a new landlord, so maybe it'll be restored to its former glory!

You reach the bar by going in through the main door and then turning right. The bar is well-lit, and quite nicely decorated. It's divided into a couple of smaller areas by seats and partitions and is big enough to seat a couple of dozen people without too much effort.

Steep-sided Ebbor Gorge is a little known jewel in the centre of the Mendips.

The beer choice is tolerable, consisting of Ushers Best, Courage Best and Founders. Founders is by far the best, unless you're thirsty and don't want to get tipsy.

It's hard to say much about the food, since the landlord was, at the time of writing, still trying to find a cook! Expect pretty standard pub fare, though.

The Wookey Hole Inn may be a bit tatty, but that can be an advantage for tired, hungry walkers. It's probably popular, too, with the local caving fraternity. The overall impression is that it's a locals pub with no airs and graces. Be warned – the bar also has a dartboard and a fruit machine.

The Wookey Hole Inn. It looks a little faded these days, but this elegant building still houses a homely bar.

Around North Wootton

Route: North Wootton – Mill Lane – Stoodly Bridge – Folly Wood

Distance: 3 miles

Start: The Crossways Inn, North Wootton (ST 566416)

By car: From Wells, take the road running south east to Dulcote. From here, take the minor road running around the southern edge of Dulcote Hill and then south down into North Wooton. The Crossways Inn is right on the crossroads in the centre of the village, and boasts a large car park.

Glastonbury Tor can be seen across the fields from Folly Lane, above North Wootton.

The Walk

North Wootton is a scattered little settlement situated in the rolling hills to the south west of Wells. This walk takes you up past North Wooton vineyards (why not drop in?) then around and up on to the high ground to the east of the village. The route down through Folly Wood and Folly Lane offers excellent views across the countryside to Glastonbury Tor and beyond.

Apart from one modest climb, it's not particularly arduous, but you may come across some mud on the bridleway through Folly Wood, depending on how much rain there's been recently, and how many hooves have churned up the ground.

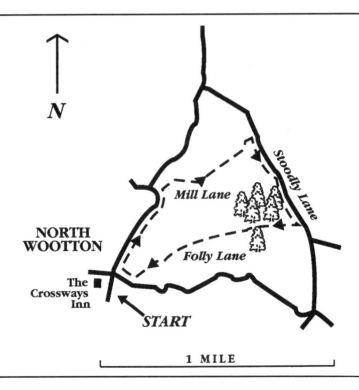

From the Crossways Inn, take the road heading north-east from the crossroads. This takes you up to Nut Tree Farm, where the main road curves round to the left but a smaller road carries on ahead. Follow this until it turns into a rough track and turns abruptly right. Just here you'll see a footpath sign, and you can either carry on in the same direction across the fields or take the track – they both end up at the same place. The fields are prettier, but the track is easier...

In 400 yards the two routes rejoin, and a little further on the track emerges on to a road (Stoodly Lane). Go right here, following the lane uphill for about 500 yards. Just as it crests the hill it starts bearing round to the left. Look out here for the bridleway leading off into the woods on the right.

Keep following the bridleway signs through Folly Wood (it can get a bit muddy here after rain). When the path emerges from the wood at a gate, follow the left-hand edge of the field beyond and go through the gate in the far left-hand corner. You now follow the right-hand edge of the field beyond, and it's from here that you get the best views on the walk.

At the next gate, aim slightly to the left of the right-hand corner of the field and you'll come to another gate and a signpost confirming you're on the right track. Once through this gate you head downhill to a metalled road. Carry on downhill and you emerge on to the road between Pilton and North Wootton. Go right here, and the Crossways Inn is a couple of hundred yards away on your left.

The Crossways Inn

This place is a little curious – it's a large hotel/restaurant/bar complex slap bang in the middle of a village hardly big enough to fill its car park! The Crossways Inn offers accommodation and conferencing facilities, so it's clearly designed to appeal to business as much as private visitors – country conferences are becoming popular these days.

There are two bars: The Crossways Lounge and the Wootton Lounge. The Crossways Lounge is much the quieter and smaller of the two. It's often so quiet, in fact, that you'll head off to the Wootton Lounge instead. 'Lounge' is not exactly the right word for this room. 'Hangar' would be more appropriate. There's space inside for a hundred people or more and it's set out more like a cafeteria than a pub (although the decor is pub-like). This is all a bit of a surprise, considering that from the outside the place looks so 'posh'.

Hungry walkers can visit the buffet bar at the end of the Wootton Lounge and partake of all the standard pub-type fare. It's not especially cheap, but the helpings are good. Kids are welcome – the menu includes a kids' section. Further investigation reveals that the Crossways Lounge and the Wootton Lounge are linked at one end by the Buffet Bar.

Beer drinkers can choose from Wadworths 6X (not bad), Bass (well-kept here) and Smiles ('safe', but not uninteresting). If you fancy a bit of the hard stuff, the place has no fewer than ten different whiskies on optics! The food and drink are basically fine, but this place does lack atmosphere. The Wootton Bar is the only bar I've seen that could accommodate several coach parties – still in their coaches. Against that, the Crossways Inn enjoys a very convenient location and it has an enormous car park. I can't imagine you'd ever be unable to park there.

The Crossways Inn, North Wootton, houses a cavernous bar with a good range of food.

Glastonbury Tor

Route: Brindham – Norwood Park – Edgarley – Glastonbury Tor

Distance: 7 or 3 miles

Start: The Waggon and Horses, Glastonbury (ST 506403)

By car: Take the A39 north out of Glastonbury towards Wells, and on the outskirts of Glastonbury you pass through the Avalon Estate. The Waggon and Horses is on the left. It has a good-sized car park, and there is roadside parking in the surrounding streets.

The Walk

Glastonbury is famous for its Tor, a striking landmark visible from many miles away. It's also surrounded by myths and legends as both the cradle of Christianity in Britain and, rather more dubiously, as the last resting place of King Arthur.

Joseph of Arimathea is believed to have come to Glastonbury in about 30-32AD. The story is that he planted his staff on Wearyall Hill, and it grew and flowered as Glastonbury Thorn. It's also said that the Holy Grail was buried at the site of the Chalice Well, at the foot of the Tor, and that afterwards this place possessed mystical healing powers. Another story has it that Joseph of Aramathea was a Mendip lead merchant, and that Jesus himself once accompanied him on a visit to Priddy.

Whatever the truth of these religious rumours, Glastonbury has been a major religious centre since Roman times. It was once a monastic community centred around the great Glastonbury Abbey, the richest and most influential abbey in the country. The monks of the Abbey were responsible for much of the land reclamation in the area. The Abbey was one of the last to be dissolved, finally falling in 1539. The building became a ruin, even a source of stone for local construction projects.

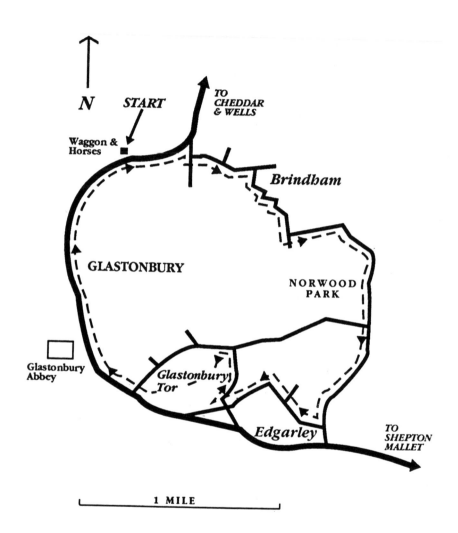

As for King Arthur, excavations have revealed some evidence that a warrior leader lived and died locally, but the rest is just supposition. Including the theory that 'Camelot' was situated at South Cadbury. Nevertheless, the legends have taken route, even turning up in place-names – the Waggon and Horses is situated on the 'Avalon' Estate.

No book about the Mendips would be complete without a visit to Glastonbury, even though the town lies to the south of the main range. The town itself boasts its fair share of historical interest, but by far the most prominent feature is the Tor ('tor' is a Celtic word meaning 'hill'), with its odd church tower at the summit. The tower is all that remains of the church of St. Michael. This was built to replace an earlier church which collapsed following an earthquake in the thirteenth century. There's evidence of earlier buildings on the summit, however, going back to the fifth or sixth centuries.

The views from the top of Glastonbury Tor are breathtaking, and well worth the short climb.

The Tor is not particularly high (518 feet), but, set as it is in the middle of flat land to the south of the main Mendip ridge, it's as striking a feature as Brent Knoll, to the west.

Having said that, it's a troublesome place for walkers. While the whole of Brent Knoll is criss-crossed by paths, Glastonbury Tor is a different kettle of fish. The central hill is owned by the National Trust, and open to the public, but the land on the surrounding plateau is heavily farmed. There are footpaths, but they're often overgrown, generally indistinct, and never go anywhere useful. Anyone wanting to tour the Tor (sorry) is pretty well confined to country roads.

That said, the road running clockwise from the northern edge of Glastonbury round to Edgarley is not busy and gives good views northwards to the Mendips as well as a generally pleasant country stroll. And there are always those tantalising glimpses of the Tor to your right. It's strange – you always have the feeling you're walking away from it, yet every time you glimpse it it's closer...

Starting from the Waggon and Horses, you head left down the (regrettably busy) main road to the edge of the town, where you see a turning off to the right just before a small bridge. You walk a few yards along this road, then turn left.

This narrow country road twists and turns all over the place, but heads generally clockwise around the Tor. Don't be tempted by any public footpath signs leading you – apparently – towards the Tor. The road is the most reliable way round, if rather less exciting!

As you walk around the Tor, you'll probably be able to make out the terraces of medieval field system on its south-eastern slopes. Some people believe these terraces form a kind of maze, that the Tor is hollow, even that it has an entrance to the underworld; there are countless legends surrounding Glastonbury, many of which can be traced back to monastic clerics with an eye for publicity – in particular the Arthurian legends.

Just as you're about to emerge on to the A361 heading west into Glastonbury, you'll see a turning on your right. Follow this narrow road uphill. You'll see the Tor tantalisingly close on your left, but you'll have to wait until you've turned left at the road junction ahead before you see the entrance to the Tor. (There are just two entrances – one here, one on the far western side.)

Whatever the tales surrounding Glastonbury and the Tor, one extremely grisly event certainly did happen here. In 1539, Richard Whiting, the last Abbot of Glastonbury, was hung, drawn and quartered on this spot. Charming.

After short climb you find yourself at the top of the Tor. The views of the surrounding countryside are excellent, and the church tower a fascinating oddity. You won't be the only one to find it fascinating, however – don't expect to get the place to yourself.

Once you've spent a few minutes taking in the vistas, you can start the descent westwards down into Glastonbury. This heads down a ridge towards the town and is equally impressive, with panoramic views over the town and beyond.

Striking though it is, Glastonbury Tor still has to give best to Brent Knoll in my opinion. Both are solitary peaks rising from flat land to give breathtaking views of the surrounding landscape. But the Tor is landlocked, only semi-rural and difficult to reach. Brent Knoll, by contrast, is unspoilt, well served by footpaths and offers the more striking vistas. That's just my opinion, though.

Once at the base of the Tor you're faced with a longish stretch back along the main road through Glastonbury town centre. This walk is as much for the history buff as the countryside lover, since it gives you the chance to divert into the town to visit the Abbey and the museum, as well as other places of interest.

For those who don't fancy tackling the full walk described above, an alternative is to park in the town centre, which is much nearer the Tor, and climb it from there.

To get back to the Waggon and Horses, keep to the A39 as it bends through and then out of Glastonbury towards Wells.

The Waggon and Horses, Glastonbury. A bit rough and ready, but a welcome sight in a town short of pubs.

The Waggon and Horses

There are posh eating-out pubs, there are pokey little country pubs, there are young, lively town pubs... and there's the Waggon and Horses. This is about as close as you can get to a traditional pub – full of smoke, boozers and raucousness.

The public bar is not especially inviting, but the lounge is marginally more comfortable. Bass and Butcombe are the beers on offer, and there's also a modest pub food menu which consists of old stalwarts like ploughman's lunches, plaice and chips and toasted sandwiches. Not the sort of place you go to eat, let's say that, but fine if you're hungry and you're there anyway.

For the warmer weather, there's a large beer garden to the rear of the pub. This is actually quite nice and much better, to be honest, than the bars. It's useful, too, for those with kids. Car parking is pretty good –

there's a fair-sized car park alongside the pub, and you shouldn't have too much trouble finding roadside parking nearby.

Overall, the Waggon and Horses is a very basic town pub, which gives it it's own perverse sort of charm. It's not especially good for beer, you wouldn't go there for meal out and it's bad news if you're not fond of passive smoking. However, Glastonbury is not well-endowed with pubs, and after finding one we can park at, eat at and walk from, we'd better consider ourselves lucky...

Introduction to the Eastern Hills

The Walks

Mells   From The Sun Inn, Whatley (ST 737474)

Nunney Combe   From The George, Nunney (ST 737457)

Holcombe Church   From The Kings Arms, Stratton-on-the-Fosse
                       (ST 657506)

The Area

By the time you get this far east, the Mendips have been 'tamed'. Gone are the dramatic vistas, forest and cliffs to the west. Instead, you are in a land of pleasant, rolling hills, picturesque villages and dusty, noisy quarries.

Sadly, many of the Mendip hills are being slowly chipped away by quarry workings. Around Mells, though, the biggest problem is not the quarry workings themselves but the quarry trucks which thunder incessantly to and fro along the country roads.

However, once away from the main roads you can easily forget about this twentieth century intrusion. The village of Mells itself is an extremely attractive place lying on the Mells Stream, which you can follow all the way to nearby Great Elm.

Meanwhile, two miles to the south is the village of Nunney, which is just as attractive and, likewise, lies on a small river. Nunney's main claim to fame is the bizarre ruined castle right in the centre of the village. It looks like a cut-down version of the real thing – complete with moat – but was in fact built long after military strategy and tactics had rendered traditional castles obsolete. It was besieged during the English Civil War, but fell with little resistance.

There is one more essential stopping-off point in this area, and that's the town of Stratton-on-the-Fosse, five miles to the west of Mells. Or rather it's not the town itself, as much as the nearby Holcombe Church, situated in an isolated woodland spot and enjoying one of the most attractive locations of any church in the region.

Mells

Route: Whatley – Chantry – Mells – Great Elm

Distance: 7 miles

Start: The Sun Inn, Whatley (ST 737474)

By car: Whatley is about 1.5 miles east of Frome, and reached via minor roads. The Sun Inn is up a short road on your left just before a sharp left-hand bend in the middle of the village. There is ample parking both in front of and at the back of the pub.

The Walk

The villages of Whatley and Mells are right at the eastern margin of the Mendips, close to the town of Frome. By now the Mendips have spread out and become a much tamer range of hills, without the dramatic vistas and climbs of the western, seaward end. However, they still offer some very pleasant country walking – despite the fact that the area is at the centre of major quarrying activities, and the roads reverberate to the thundering of heavily-laden quarry trucks.

This noisy industrial development is a shame, because the village of Mells is a charming little rural settlement, and the picturesque and secluded Mells Stream makes for some great walking.

The early part of this walk takes place on country roads, skirting the massive (and expanding) quarry east of Whatley. Soon the route descends into picturesque Mells village. From here, the route follows the edge of the river, then climbs to return to the Sun Inn across the fields. Despite the moderate length of this walk, it's not particularly taxing, and there's plenty to see.

From the Sun Inn, walk back down to the road and turn left. Carry on along this road, following it round to the left and then uphill to a

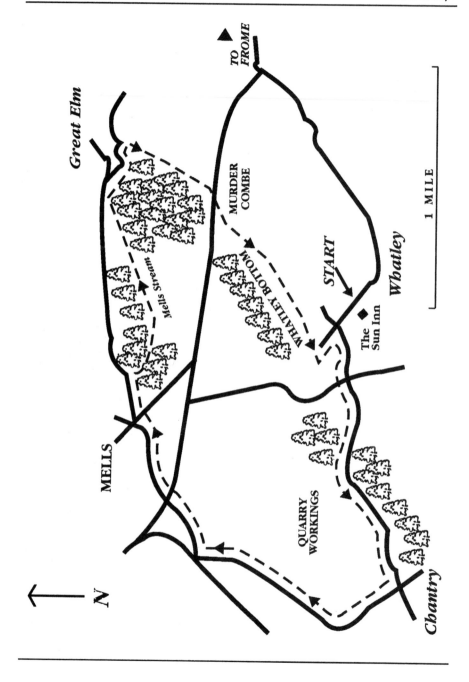

Mells Stream opens out into a picturesque little lake at Great Elm.

crossroads. Go straight over and carry on along this road for nearly a mile before reaching the village of Chantry. If you have a map, you may be tempted to try a path from Railford Bridge (half way between Whatley and Chantry) which leads behind Little Acre farm to join the Chantry – Mells road. Try it if you like, but it saves little time and gets very overgrown in the summer.

From Chantry, follow the road to Mells northwards. After a mile you reach another crossroads, Turn right here to descend into picturesque Mells village.

Mells was once owned by the all-powerful Glastonbury Abbey, and developed as a cloth-making centre. From the mid-eighteenth to the mid-nineteenth century, though, it was an industrial centre. The same water that had powered the woollen industry in previous centuries now powered the Fussell edge-tool works on the banks of the Mells Stream. The ruins are still there today, even though they're overgrown and largely hidden until you're right on top of them.

Go straight across at the next crossroads and pretty soon the road turns sharply to the left to cross Mells Stream. Go right now, and take the Great Elm road, which follows the edge of the river. About 300 yards along this road you'll see a layby to your right. There's a gate here which leads on to a path following the edge of the river.

This path follows the river bank all the way to Great Elm. The walking here is pleasant and relaxing, and yet fascinating too. Half way between Mells and Great Elm are the ruins of the Fussell factory. As you reach the ruins the path forks left and right. The right fork takes you in amongst the ruins, but you'll have to retrace your steps to continue the walk. The left hand fork takes you round the ruins and on to Great Elm.

A little further the path joins a rather grand walk-way running through a well-kept grassy area below equally well-kept houses on the hillside above. On the other side of this open stretch the route divides again. The upper route (going off to the left) is a bridleway. This isn't the one we want. Instead, we want the public footpath which heads off the right.

The track now is quite narrow, but sticks to the side of the river. You know you're nearing Great Elm when it begins climbing uphill and away from the river. You then join a narrow road which proceeds downhill and then turns sharp right across the river. At this point you get possibly the best view of the walk, an idyllic waterscape of millpond-like stillness, overhanging trees and the gentle sound of trickling water.

Having taken in this view (and perhaps a packet of sandwiches) you now carry on up the road, with the aim of turning right to head south west back to Whatley. Now as soon as you start up this road you'll see a gate on your right and a stile. Ignore this. Carry on up the road for another 50-100 yards and you'll see another signpost (labelled Shepton Mallet). This is the path you want. A few yards up this path the track bears right and from here it's plain (if occasionally overgrown) sailing uphill to Murder Combe where you have to cross a road. The path carries on directly opposite (facing you, slightly to your left). This takes you into a field. You follow the left-hand edge until you come to another stile, then stick to the right-hand edge of the next field, climbing gently, and heading for the right-hand corner of the field as you crest the rise. This corner looks like it's full of nothing but long grass, nettles and thistles, but as you draw nearer you'll see a stile right in the corner. Once over this stile, you'll see another still ahead of you. Climb over this one, then head diagonally across to your left, towards a partly-concealed footpath between the houses. This leads you down a track, past more houses, to the road running through Whatley. You'll see the Sun Inn to your left as you emerge.

The Sun Inn

The Sun Inn is a really colourful country pub – it's great for families too. Inside, there are two bars; the main lounge bar/restaurant, and a smaller public bar. The lounge bar is large enough for a couple of dozen people, and is bright, airy and open. It's also tastefully decorated. The restaurant is at the back of the lounge in a separate room.

The range of draught beers is limited, but interesting – the two on offer at the time of writing were Salisbury Bitter and Wiltshire Bitter, which are new ones on me.

If the choice of beers is fairly restricted, the menu isn't! This is a gargantuan affair printed on a large A3 sheet and decorated with 'helpful' illustrations (Shoulder of Lamb is indicated with a drawing of a sheep and an arrow!). There should be something here for all tastes, including Tex-Mex (chilli and tortillas), duck breast and other exotic dishes. And there are some desserts on offer that you may have thought had gone forever, including treacle pudding and spotted dick.

The Sun Inn is OK for beer, then and great for food. It's also a terrific 'summer evening pub', with a very pleasant garden complete with half a dozen benches and tables. The car park is a good size, too (in fact there are two of them, front and rear), so finding a space shouldn't be a problem even at busy times. And children are welcome in all the bars, too.

The Sun Inn, Whatley. Very 'sunny' indeed, with good food, good beer and great surroundings.

Nunney Combe

Route: Nunney Castle – Nunney Brook – Nunney Combe

Distance: 2.5 miles

Start: The George, Nunney (ST 737457)

By car: From Frome, take the A361 south west. Nunney is reached via a turn-off to the right about two miles outside the town. The George is half way along the main street, and has a small car park facing it on the opposite side of the road. There is another small car park outside some shops a little way down the road, beyond that only limited roadside parking.

The Walk

The main attraction of Nunney is its ruined castle, but this little village also boasts a very attractive duckpond alongside the main street. It's also a good starting point for walks around the local countryside, including this one, which explores the secluded Nunney Combe.

Nunney Castle saw only brief military action and quickly fell to its attackers.

There are no real hills, but the prospect of some mud on the walk through the Combe depending, as ever, on the weather. The castle has to be the first port of call, though. It dominates the centre of the village, although it's not in itself all that large – but it does have a moat!

Actually, the castle is a bit of a cheat. It's more of a fortified mansion than a true castle, and its design was already out of date as far as current military strategy was concerned when it was built, in 1373. The builder was Sir John De-La-Mer, and his 'castle' consisted of a central block with four corner towers. The servants lived on the ground floor, where the kitchens and stores were, while the first floor consisted of the servants' hall and 'service rooms'. The great hall was on the second floor. The only military action it saw was a short siege in the Civil War, when it proved a pretty ineffective stronghold and was promptly overrun.

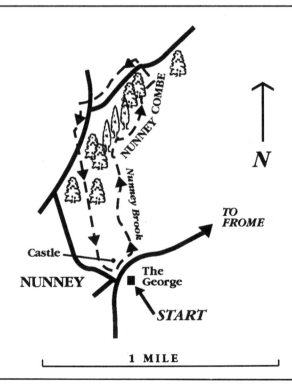

From the George, head right (north east) up the main street. You pass a church on your right and a duckpond on the left. A few yards further on, a road branches off to the left. Follow this road to its end and a gateway leading to Combe Farm, and a Public Footpath signpost. Follow this path and then, when it curves round to the left, keep going straight ahead, climbing over the stile facing you. This path leads you alongside Nunney Brook and into the tree-lined Nunney Combe. After rain, you may come across some mud, but nothing too serious.

After half a mile of this, you'll come to a small clearing where a metalled track comes in from the left. Now in principle you should be able to carry on along the banks of the river. This route is obstructed, though, so you have to go left here, crossing the brook and then climbing uphill to emerge on the road near Lower Whatley.

Now go left along the road. This soon brings you to a T-junction, where you again turn left. This road is pretty busy, so you'll be glad of the chance to get off it and cross the fields back to Nunney. You get this chance just after a dip in the road, about 300 yards from the junction. In the bottom of this dip, on your left, is a big metal gate. A few yards further on is a smaller gate. This is the one you want. Climb over the gate and then strike out diagonally across the field towards the line of trees facing you – aim for the telegraph pole. Once through the trees, aim diagonally across towards the far left-hand corner of the field (aim for the church). Once over this stile, follow the left-hand edge of the field beyond to another stile.

The track then carries on down into Nunney, emerging just before the main T-junction in the village. Turn left at this junction and you'll see the George just a few yards up the road.

The George

The main street through Nunney is old and quaint, and the George, half way along it, looks older and quainter. But if you're expecting a poky little stone-floored spit 'n' sawdust pub you're in for a surprise – inside, it's large and rather posh. The ceilings are low, the interior gloomy but grand. On the left is the main bar, while on the right is a small area for families. The bar is set out for eating with space for two or three dozen people. You walk through it to reach the equivalent of the public bar/games room. At the back of the George is a restaurant. (Accommodation is available too.)

The beers on offer include Bass, 6X and Butcombe – a decent enough choice, but not as decent as the range of single-malt whiskies available. At the last count there were fifteeen!

As far as food is concerned, steaks are clearly something of a speciality. Most sizes and cuts are available, and all at very reasonable prices indeed. Most spectacular is the 32oz. T-bone, which costs £11.50. The menu also includes all the normal pub fare. It's not particularly cheap, but the George is quite an upmarket pub. In fact it's the sort of place you would go for an evening out. It's also a great place to visit after a walk, but don't tramp in muddy boots and expect a warm welcome!

Parking is a bit of a nightmare, though. There are a few spaces directly across the road, but you'd have to get their quite early to be sure of getting one. A little further along the road there are more spaces by the local shops, but beyond that you'll have to settle for whatever roadside parking you can find nearby.

The George, Nunney. A great choice of steaks, and an even greater choice of whiskies!

Holcombe Church

Route: Stratton-on-the-Fosse – Moore's Farm – Holcombe

Distance: 3 miles

Start: The Kings Arms, Stratton-on-the-Fosse (ST 657506)

By car: Take the A37 north from Shepton Mallet then turn on to the A367 just before Oakhill. Stratton-on-the-Fosse is about three miles further on, and the Kings Arms is on the right, soon after you enter the village. There is a modest car park next to the pub, and limited roadside parking on the streets nearby.

The Walk

This walk is quite short, and shouldn't pose problems for anyone, following, for the most part, quiet country lanes. The main attraction is the beautiful and secluded little church in Holcombe Wood.

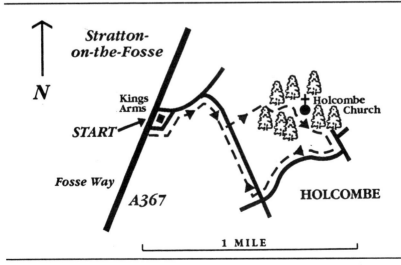

Holcombe Church enjoys one of the most picturesque locations on the Mendips.

Follow the road that runs downhill alongside the Kings Arms. This leads downhill for a short distance, then curves left and rises gently to head past a church. A few yards further on a road leads off to the right. Follow this down into a dip then uphill and to the right. A little further on, on your left, you'll see a broad track leading off to the left, together with a footpath sign (if it's not completely hidden by vegetation).

You head through a stile and then a gate to the field next to Holcombe Wood. Cut across diagonally to the right towards the trees and you'll see a narrow footpath heading into Holcombe Wood.

This path meanders gently downhill until, at the bottom of the descent, you reach a gate on your left and a set of shallow steps uphill to your right. Follow the steps upwards and you soon emerge from the woods at a stile. You're now at Holcombe church, one of the most secluded and picturesque churches on the Mendips.

Follow the churchyard wall and you come to a metalled track leading towards Holcombe village. Then follow this track as it curves left then right through Moore's Farm. Once past the farm, ignore the first turning on your right, but then turn right when you arrive at a T-junction.

The road now leads south through the village of Holcombe, until you reach a crossroads. Turn right here, and follow the road as it heads west, then north. Thirsty walkers should note there's a supplementary watering hole here...

Carry straight on over the next crossroads and you'll soon recognise the road you used earlier, with the turn-off towards Holcombe wood now passing you by on your right. You now retrace your steps, heading uphill and then left back to the Kings Arms.

The Kings Arms

Don't expect to find the Kings Arms in any Egon Ronay guide. It's a basic village pub with modest decor, modest beers and a modest menu. The main bar is the Fosse Bar, and it's pretty rough and ready, but still comfortable enough. To the right is a snooker room and elsewhere is a dining room, for those who find the bar a bit too basic.

The beer choice includes Ushers Best, Courage Best and Founders. The two 'Bests' are, actually 'worsts' – the Founders is by far the best of the three. The food is standard pub grub – and everything was £2.95 in 1992. There's also a 'specials' board featuring a handful of basic home-made dishes.

There's nothing much here for kids, whether or not they're allowed inside, but there is a moderately large car park, so parking should be easy enough.

It's often the case that the most attractive areas offer the least choice in pubs – and vice versa. It would be a shame to miss out the countryside around Stratton-on-the-Fosse and especially Holcombe Church, though, and the Kings Arms is a reasonable enough pub to retire to after a walk through the countryside.

The Kings Arms, Stratton-on-the-Fosse. Rather basic, but good value.

Explore the countryside with Sigma!

We have a wide selection of guides to individual towns, plus outdoor activities centred on walking and cycling in the great outdoors throughout England and Wales. This is a recent selection:

PEAK DISTRICT DIARY – Roger Redfern
An evocative book, celebrating the glorious countryside of the Peak District. The book is based on Roger's popular column in *The Guardian* newspaper and is profusely illustrated with stunning photographs. *£6.95*

I REMAIN, YOUR SON JACK – J. C. Morten (edited by Sheila Morten)
A collection of almost 200 letters, as featured on BBC TV, telling the moving story of a young soldier in the First World War. Profusely illustrated with contemporary photographs. *£8.95*

There are many books for outdoor people in our catalogue, including:

RAMBLES IN NORTH WALES
– Roger Redfern

HERITAGE WALKS IN THE PEAK DISTRICT
– Clive Price

EAST CHESHIRE WALKS
– Graham Beech

WEST CHESHIRE WALKS
– Jen Darling

WEST PENNINE WALKS
– Mike Cresswell

NEWARK AND SHERWOOD RAMBLES
– Malcolm McKenzie

RAMBLES AROUND NOTTINGHAM & DERBY
– Keith Taylor

RAMBLES AROUND MANCHESTER
– Mike Cresswell

WESTERN LAKELAND RAMBLES
– Gordon Brown

WELSH WALKS:
Dolgellau and the Cambrian Coast
– Laurence Main and Morag Perrott

WELSH WALKS:
Aberystwyth and District
– Laurence Main and Morag Perrott

– all of these books are currently £6.95 each.

NOTES

NOTES